THE LIAR

THE KINGSWOOD PLAYS

THE LIAR

by

CARLO GOLDONI

Translated and Adapted

by

FREDERICK H. DAVIES

From the Carlo Signorelli Edition of
Il Bugiardo

HEINEMANN EDUCATIONAL BOOKS

LONDON

Heinemann Educational Books Ltd
22 Bedford Square, London WC1B 3HH

LONDON EDINBURGH MELBOURNE AUCKLAND
HONG KONG SINGAPORE KUALA LUMPUR NEW DELHI
IBADAN NAIROBI JOHANNESBURG KINGSTON
EXETER (NH) PORT OF SPAIN

ISBN 0 435 21013 0

Reproduced, printed and bound in Great Britain by
Fakenham Press Limited, Fakenham, Norfolk

INTRODUCTION

TO THE BOYS AND GIRLS WHO
WILL ACT IN THIS PLAY

'Goldoni – good, gay, sunniest of souls, –
Glassing half Venice in that verse of thine, –
. . . Dear King of Comedy,
Be honoured! thou that didst love Venice so, –
Venice, and we who love her, all love thee!'

So wrote our English poet Robert Browning – who loved
Venice, lived there for many years, and died there in his
palazzo on the Grand Canal – when Carlo Goldoni's statue
was unveiled.

If you wander down the busy Merceria, the 'Regent Street'
of Venice, you will come to that statue. There he stands today,
the man who wrote this and over a hundred other comedies,
smiling quizzically down at the Venetians of the twentieth
century.

Who was he, this Carlo Goldoni? He is so little known in
our country. And yet to Italians he is what Shakespeare is to
Englishmen. He is the *Gran Goldoni*. And to the children of
Venice, as to their fathers and mothers, he is still *papà Goldoni*.

He was born in Venice on 25 February 1707. He died in
Paris during the French Revolution, on 6 February 1793,
only a few days after Louis XVI was taken to the guillotine.
For forty-six of those eighty-six years of his life, Carlo
Goldoni was ceaselessly writing plays for the theatres of Italy
and France. During one of these years, in order to save the
theatre in Venice for which he was working from having to

close down, he made a rash promise that he would write sixteen plays in one year. He wrote afterwards in his Memoirs: 'It was a terrible year for me, which I cannot recall without trembling.'

The wonder is that Goldoni did not die in his attempt to keep that rash promise. For keep it he did. He had set himself the stupendous physical task of writing the equivalent of five modern novels in one year. How he kept that promise is best told by Goldoni himself:

Only one play remained to be written to fulfil my promise to my Venetian public. We had reached the last Sunday but one of the season and I had not written a single line of the sixteenth play. I left my house for a walk about St Mark's Square. I kept looking about for something – anything – which might supply me with a subject for the sixteenth play. Then, under the arcade of the clock-tower, I saw him, the man who was to provide me with the subject I was looking for. He was an old, dirty, poorly dressed Armenian who went about the streets of Venice selling dried fruit which he called *abagigi*. This man was so well known and so much laughed at, that when anyone wanted to tease a girl looking for a husband, they suggested she should marry Abagigi.

I needed no more. I went back to my house, shut myself up in my room, and began the comedy which I called *The Women's Gossip*. With it we closed the season. The audience was so large that we had to double and treble the price of the boxes, and the applause was so long and loud that passers-by wondered whether a riot was taking place. I sat quietly in my box. Then crowds of people came and dragged me out and began paying me compliments which I would have been glad to have avoided.

I was tired and really a little vexed that they should seem

to be placing this play so much higher than others which I had written and thought better. Gradually, however, the truth dawned upon me: they were really acclaiming the triumph of my having kept my promise, of having done what I had said I would do.

In the short space of this introduction it is not possible to tell you nearly as much as I should like to about Carlo Goldoni. This incident will perhaps have given you some idea of the sort of man he was. He achieved fame through facing and overcoming many, many difficulties; and yet he remained to the end of his long and hard life one of the most lovable and courageous of men. In his Memoirs he tells us of the happy day, when, as a young man, he brought his lovely bride home to Venice. When he died in Paris, old, in poverty, and blind in one eye, that bride was still at his side, his deeply devoted wife to the very end of his long life.

TO THE PRODUCER

The following suggestions, arising from a most successful and enjoyable production of this play with twelve- to fifteen-year-old secondary modern boys, may be found of value.

The play will probably require a little longer, or a little more intensive, period of rehearsals than is usually given to school plays, since its successful production depends upon a certain pace being attained.

Many of the lines are so short – giving the effect of quick repartee – that I found it better to discourage the learning of lines until well over half-way through rehearsals. By doing this, the boys gradually, and without realizing it, memorized the movements and lines together. For when they were at last told that they must do without their scripts by a certain date, they found that they practically knew their parts already through constant repetition.

Timing of cues and 'pointing' of words assume, of course, a greater importance in a fast comedy like this. The relation of the timing of cues to the obtaining of necessary pace is often completely misunderstood by boys, and they constantly had to be reminded at first that pace is *not* obtained by gabbling their lines quickly but simply by being very quick on their cues.

As the events of the play take place during Carnival time in Venice, an appropriate atmosphere may be created by opening the play with a short acrobatic display by half a dozen of the school gymnasts in the guise of Italian tumblers clad in red tights and white blouses. If this is done, the first entrance of LELIO and ARLECCHINO may be arranged thus:

The Carnival music[1] begins just before the curtain opens so that the team of tumblers is discovered already in action centre stage. Watching and applauding them are BRIGHELLA and the waiter (right); ROSAURA, BEATRICE and COLUMBINA (in the loggetta); OTTAVIO (beside the loggetta); and two or three of the minor characters (backstage).

At the beginning of this scene the stage is brightly-lit. About half-way through it, the lights begin gradually to dim. Just before they do so, LELIO and ARLECCHINO enter back right and cross to PANTALONE'S door. LELIO knocks. ARLECCHINO stands watching the tumblers. The door is opened. LELIO pulls ARLECCHINO inside after him and the door closes.

When the tumblers finish their act, quiet romantic music[2] begins and they line up bowing to their audience on the stage and to the audience in the hall. One of the tumblers

---

[1] Suitable music, during which a series of gymnastic pyramids may be formed, is 'Via Amalfi' on the L.P. record GGL 0043

[2] 'Venice and You' on the same record might be used.

meanwhile is taking a collection from the stage audience. The tumblers go off. Their stage audience take farewell of one another. The stage is left empty and moon-lit. A bell strikes eight. LELIO and ARLECCHINO come out of PANTALONE's house, and the play begins.

All stage directions given are from the point of view of the actors and not of the audience.

Ideal material for the construction of the framework of the loggetta is 'Roften Slotted-Angle' (trade-mark) steel scaffolding. In order to facilitate the final exit of Columbina, Pantalone and Cleonice, three abreast, it will be advisable to make the entrance to the inn fairly wide and to cover it with some form of beaded curtain.

Finally, it should perhaps be mentioned that I allowed myself considerable freedom in the translating and adapting of *The Liar*: this was necessary for its production with school children and in order to re-arrange the action for one set only. What cuts have been made have been balanced by enlarging the part of Arlecchino with some pantomimic excerpts from *Arlequin Empereur dans la Lune* which first entered the repertoire of the troupe of Italian *Commedia dell' Arte* players in Paris in 1684.

TO THE AUDIENCE
(Suggested Programme Note)

Several of Goldoni's plays show Pantalone, a respectable merchant of Venice, at his wits' end trying to keep in order either a badly-behaved son or daughter. In this play it is a son, Lelio, whose glib tongue is continually running away with him.

Pantalone has not seen his son for ten years, for Lelio went to live with an aunt and uncle in Naples on the death of his mother when he was nine years old. The play begins with the return of Lelio, now a young man of nineteen, to Venice, accompanied by his servant Arlecchino. He finds that his father is away on business, and as it is Carnival time in Venice he decides to enjoy himself while he can.

Unaware that his father has arranged a marriage for him with Rosaura the daughter of Doctor Balanzoni, Lelio introduces himself to Rosaura as the Count Fernando, Marquis of Castel d'Oro. This 'witty invention', as Lelio calls it, is the beginning of a series of complications made much more complicated –

(*i*) by Arlecchino, who tries to imitate his master's 'witty inventions' and only finds himself plunging into ridiculous lies from which he cannot extricate himself.

(*ii*) by Ottavio, who repeats as the truth all the 'witty inventions' that Lelio tells him and is himself taken to be the liar.

(*iii*) by Florindo, whose exaggerated shyness leads him unintentionally to give foundation to the 'witty inventions' of Lelio.

(*iv*) by Rosaura and Beatrice, who both want to get married before the other and so fall too easily for Lelio's 'witty inventions' and by the fact that Lelio, having been away for so long, is not recognized even by his own father.

This play is used as a school book by Italian boys and girls in the *Scuole Medie* when they are 13 to 14 years of age. The actual edition they use has a note which ends as follows:

'*Although this play has its own instructive little moral to give i.e. – honesty is always the best policy, it is nevertheless not a play for those who require an obvious moral from their literature, because it is essentially a light comedy, sparklingly vivacious from beginning to end and without a single trace of uncharitableness. What moves the strings of the characters and plot is the kindly, smiling good-nature of Carlo Goldoni.*'

THE PLAYERS IN ORDER
OF APPEARANCE

CARNIVAL ACROBATS
LELIO, son of Pantalone
ARLECCHINO, servant to Lelio
FLORINDO, a medical student from Bologna, studying with
    Doctor Balanzoni, and timidly in love with Rosaura
BRIGHELLA, aged servant to Florindo
ROSAURA, elder daughter of Doctor Balanzoni
BEATRICE, younger daughter of Doctor Balanzoni
COLUMBINA, maidservant to Rosaura and Beatrice
OTTAVIO, a gentleman from Padua, in love with Beatrice
A DRAPER'S BOY
PANTALONE DEI BISOGNOSI, a Venetian merchant and
    father of Lelio
SERVANT TO PANTALONE
DOCTOR BALANZONI, father of Rosaura and Beatrice
SERVANT TO THE DOCTOR
A NEAPOLITAN COACH DRIVER
A WAITER FROM THE EAGLE INN
A LETTER CARRIER
CLEONICE ANSELMI, a wealthy young lady from Rome,
    betrothed to Lelio unknown to his father

ACT I

SCENE I: Evening
SCENE II: The following morning

ACT II

SCENE I: Afternoon of the same day
SCENE II: Late afternoon of the same day

The scene throughout is a corner of a square in Venice in the eighteenth century. On the right are the houses of Pantalone and Doctor Balanzoni. Doctor Balanzoni's is nearest the audience, and has a *loggetta*. An Italian *loggetta* is a kind of small veranda, but differs from a veranda in being more architectural, and in forming more decidedly a part of the main building. On the left is the Eagle Inn.

NOTES ON CHARACTERS

LELIO: A young gallant, handsome, debonair and elegant; in manner and dress a little larger than life. His ingenuous charm should prevent his many extravagances from alienating the sympathy of the audience.

ARLECCHINO: Quick of repartee and sprightly in movement. Although incorrigibly knavish, he has the sense to see where Lelio's extravagances will lead that young man. Arlecchino's many asides should establish a friendly bond between himself and the audience. Descended from Harlequin of the *Commedia dell' Arte*, he wears the traditional multi-coloured, diamond-shaped, baggy trousers. One side of the brim of his hat should be turned up with a rabbit's tail or small feather stuck in it. Wears a bright yellow tunic, with a wide black belt to which is suspended a short black baton.

PANTALONE: Pompous and mercenary, traditionally tall and thin with a pointed grey beard. Dressed completely in red, edged with white fur or silver lamé; close-fitting doublet, breeches, stockings and slippers turned up at toes. Loose pointed red cape. Walks with a silver-headed stick.

DOCTOR BALANZONI: Pompous and fussy, traditionally short and fat with a pointed grey beard. Dressed completely in black, with white collar and black cloak. Round black hat with wide brim. Breeches and stockings. Walks with a cane.

FLORINDO: Timid and shy only in the presence of Rosaura, otherwise impetuous and aggressive. The excesses of his adoration make him faintly comic in spite of his romantic air. Wears eighteenth-century costume and sword.

BRIGHELLA: A cheerful old rough diamond. Also wears eighteenth-century costume.

ROSAURA and BEATRICE: Typical lively girls looking for an opportunity to rebel against the strictness of their Venetian bourgeois upbringing. Both lack Columbina's common sense.

COLUMBINA: Vivacious, outspoken, coquettish, quick-tempered.

OTTAVIO: Very self-confident. Slightly priggish. Aggressive in his friendliness to Florindo and in his animosity (later) to Lelio.

CLEONICE: Completely self-assured. Should leave the impression that, in her, Lelio has met his match – and his salvation.

ACT I

Scene I

*The scene is a street corner in Venice. On the right is the Eagle Inn.
Down right, by the Inn door, are a table and chair. On the left are the
houses of* PANTALONE *and* DR BALANZONI. *Back stage there
is a bridge (not used) crossing a canal, beyond which is a backcloth
representing the houses on the other side of the canal. The Doctor's
house is nearest the audience and has a small loggetta.*

*After an introductory Carnival scene (see note to Producer) the
stage is silent, empty and moon-lit. A bell strikes eight.* LELIO
and ARLECCHINO *come out of* PANTALONE'S *house.*

LELIO (*coming centre stage*): Well, that settles it. We'll stay at
  this Inn for a couple of days. (*He gestures towards Eagle Inn
  on right.*)
ARLECCHINO (*following him centre*): I still think it would be
  better to stay here in your father's house. (*He gestures
  towards the door out of which they have just come.*)
LELIO: But you heard what my father's housekeeper said.
  My father's out of town! Oh, I'll go and stay with him all
  right, when he gets back. (*Laughs ruefully.*) I'll have
  to!
ARLECCHINO: So in the meantime you're going to put up
  at this here Inn?
LELIO: Well, why shouldn't I enjoy my liberty while I'm
  still able to? Anyway, I've been away from Venice for ten

years, so I want to see something of it while I can. Come, bring my trunk into the Inn – before that coachman who drove us here from Naples finds us again. (*Goes towards Inn.*) Though I think we've given him the slip all right this time. (*Goes into Inn.*)

ARLECCHINO (*lifting trunk and carrying it towards the Inn*): I shouldn't be too sure of that, if I was you. These Neapolitan drivers like to see the colour of their money. (*Goes into the Inn.*)

> *Soft music begins and* ROSAURA *and* BEATRICE *come out into the loggetta and seat themselves. They make mock conversation for a few moments.* FLORINDO *appears back-stage right. He turns and calls impatiently to* BRIGHELLA *off-stage to hurry up. He begins to cross left to the Doctor's door when he sees* ROSAURA *and* BEATRICE. *He halts, petrified with shyness.* BRIGHELLA *hobbles on stage behind him, back right.* FLORINDO *turns, seizes* BRIGHELLA *by the arm and pulls him well down stage right.*

FLORINDO: Look, Brighella, there's my darling Rosaura in the loggetta with Beatrice. Let us enter by the side door, so that we don't disturb them.

BRIGHELLA: I've never seen such a strange young man as you are, Signor Florindo. You've got me fair puzzled. Here you are, studying to be a doctor with her father – living in the same house as she does – and yet you never once open your mouth to the Signora Rosaura.

FLORINDO: My dear Brighella, you know I've already told you it's no use. I just haven't got the courage. If I were to *speak* to my darling Rosaura, I know I'd simply die of blushing.

BRIGHELLA: You should try taking a lesson from Signor Ottavio. He don't let the grass grow under his feet where the Signora *Beatrice* is concerned.

FLORINDO: But *I* am *not* Signor Ottavio and I'm *not* in love with the Signora Beatrice.

BRIGHELLA: Look, young master. I was serving your father before you was born. And when I look at you now, I sees your father standing before me again, as he was himself thirty years gone by. And it's for his sake you're right welcome to any help I can give you.

FLORINDO: Yes, yes, I know, that, Brighella! So, do as I say, there's a good chap, and let us go in by the side door. (*He goes off back left.*)

BRIGHELLA: Have it your own way, then. But it fair beats me where you think this dilly-dallying will ever get you! (*Follows him.*)

    LELIO *and* ARLECCHINO *come out of the Inn and stand in spot left-centre stage.*

LELIO: Well, Arlecchino, what d'you think of Venice, eh? Just the place for a bit of fun, what?

ARLECCHINO: Aye – so long as there's a bit of eating thrown in as well.

LELIO: We'll have a good meal later on. I want to have a look round first and see what's going on. Ho, ho! I think we've found something already. Look at those two girls over there. It's rather dark to tell properly, but I'd say they're a couple of real beauties!

ARLECCHINO: Aye – they're all beauties to you – for a time. What about the Signora Cleonice in Rome only last week? *She* fair dazzled you, and now you've left her.

LELIO: *And* forgotten her. We're not in Rome now, Arlecchino. We're in Venice, and in that loggetta are two young ladies, who – and I'm not usually mistaken in this – are waiting for somebody just like me to come along and admire them. Anyhow, there's no harm in trying my luck.

ARLECCHINO: By which you mean, I suppose, that you're going to tell them the usual ten lies to every four words!

LELIO: Don't be impertinent! All the same, perhaps it would be best to find out who they are before I speak to them. Yes, you go back into the Inn and see if you can find out who they are and what their names are.

ARLECCHINO: Here we go again! (*Goes into the Inn.*)

LELIO (*walking up and down outside the Inn*): Yes – I'm just feeling in the mood for a new adventure.

 The spot on LELIO *is dimmed and the light in the loggetta is brought up slightly.* LELIO *sits at the Inn table right. He should not look across at the girls, but can occasionally glance round impatiently at the Inn door.*

ROSAURA: Oh, Beatrice, how I wish some nice young man would pay me compliments – like Signor Ottavio does to you.

BEATRICE: Well, what about Signor Florindo? I'm quite sure he's a secret admirer of yours. You know, you should encourage him a little more.

ROSAURA: But I do try to, I do really. Several times recently I've spoken quite nicely to him, but you'd think he was a woman-hater the way he ignores me.

BEATRICE: Sister! I think there's a young man over there – by the Inn!

ROSAURA: Yes, I know! He's been there a few minutes, now. Oh, dear! I wonder if he's going to speak to us!

 Spot comes up slightly on LELIO.

LELIO (*rising from chair by Inn table*): Arlecchino's a long time. I'd like to make sure of the best way to go about this. Still, I can keep to generalities until he comes back.

ROSAURA: I'm sure he's going to speak to us! Let's go in!

BEATRICE: Oh! Don't be silly! What are you frightened of?

LELIO (*swaggering centre stage and speaking with affected 'panache'*):

Oh, what a wonderful evening! Oh, what a glorious night! (*Turns towards loggetta.*) Ah! The heavens indeed shine bright when they are lit by two such delightful stars!

ROSAURA (*to* BEATRICE): He means us!

BEATRICE (*to* ROSAURA): The man's mad!

LELIO (*making a flourishing bow*): Might I dare to be so bold as to venture to wish you two ladies a very good evening?

ROSAURA: You honour us, sir.

LELIO: You are enjoying the evening air in your loggetta?

BEATRICE: We are enjoying a little liberty during our father's absence.

LELIO (*approaching the loggetta*): Ah, your honoured father is out of town, then?

ROSAURA: Yes, sir.

BEATRICE: Are you, then, acquainted with our father, sir?

LELIO (*returning centre stage*): Oh, yes! Yes, indeed! Your father is a great friend of mine. Might I make so bold as to ask where he has gone.

ROSAURA: He has gone to Padua. To visit a rich patient of his.

LELIO (*aside*): Ah, a doctor! (*Aloud.*) Yes, your father is indeed a doctor in a million! Always looking after his patients. Never thinks of himself. He is truly a great man!

ROSAURA: It is very kind of you to say so. You appear to know all about *us*, sir. May we ask who you are?

LELIO: I? I am merely a humble admirer of your charms.

ROSAURA: Of mine, sir?

LELIO (*mysteriously*): Of those of one of you!

BEATRICE: Pray, sir, cannot you be a little more explicit?

LELIO: I must, alas, keep that a secret for the moment.

    ARLECCHINO *comes out of the Inn. The light in the loggetta dims slightly.* ROSAURA *and* BEATRICE *whisper together excitedly during the following.*

ARLECCHINO (*looking around*): Now where's he got to?
> LELIO *goes over to him and takes him by the arm down right.*
LELIO (*aside to* ARLECCHINO): Well? Have you found out
who they are?
ARLECCHINO (*aside to* LELIO): Ho – Ho! Ho – ho! I know
everything! The waiters have told me everything!
LELIO: Well, quickly then!
ARLECCHINO: In the first place, you'd better know that
they're the daughters of a certain . . .
LELIO (*interrupting him brusquely*): Their names! What are
their names!
ARLECCHINO: Take your time, sir! This is important. Their
father's a doctor!
LELIO: I know that already, you dolt! Tell me their names,
you imbecile!
ARLECCHINO: One's Rosaura and the other's Beatrice.
(*Mutters.*) A wonder you haven't found that out!
> *Light comes up again slightly in loggetta.*
LELIO (*returning to the loggetta*): Oh, do excuse me, but I had
given my servant an urgent commission to execute.
ROSAURA: Sir, we are a little puzzled. Are you a Venetian, or
are you on a visit to Venice?
LELIO: Alas, I am merely visiting Venice. I am a Neapolitan
nobleman.
ARLECCHINO (*aside – to the audience – down right*): Three lies
at one go!
ROSAURA: How is it that you know us then?
LELIO: My visit has been quite a long one. As a matter of fact
I have been staying incognito in Venice for nearly a year
now.
ARLECCHINO (*aside – down right*): We arrived this evening!
LELIO: However, hardly had I arrived here – when my eyes
beheld the charms of the Signora *Rosaura* and the Signora

Beatrice. Ever since – for twelve long months – I have been in doubt. Upon which of them should I bestow my heart?

ROSAURA (*with excitement*): And now – have you decided?

LELIO: I have indeed. But, alas, I must not say which!

ARLECCHINO (*aside*): If he gets the chance, he'll tell the same tale to both of 'em.

ROSAURA: Why ever not, sir?

LELIO: Because I fear I may have left it too late, and she whom I favour may have chosen another!

ROSAURA (*quickly*): Oh, I can assure you, sir, that I am not promised to anyone.

BEATRICE: Nor I, sir!

ARLECCHINO: Two of 'em, at one go! Just his luck!

ROSAURA: At least, sir, you may tell us your name?

LELIO: With pleasure. I am the – Count Fernando, Marquis of Castel d'Oro.

ARLECCHINO (*aside*): And Emperor of Bongo-wongo land!
   LELIO *walks nonchalantly right to* ARLECCHINO *and raises his arm threateningly; he is returning, still with affected composure, centre stage just as the girls finish the following asides.*

BEATRICE (*aside to* ROSAURA): We had better be going in, or he'll be thinking we're only common people!

ROSAURA (*aside to* BEATRICE): You're right! Such a great nobleman must be accustomed to prudent behaviour in young ladies! (*Aloud, with some affectation.*) My lord marquis, with your permission – the air is becoming somewhat chilly. (*Both girls stand.*)

LELIO (*taken aback*): You're not going in already?

BEATRICE (*also somewhat affectedly*): Our old nurse is calling, sir, and we must obey.

ARLECCHINO (*aside*): Patience! There's always tomorrow!

ROSAURA: We shall meet again, my lord.

LELIO: With your permission, I shall call upon you to-morrow.

BEATRICE: Oh, no, sir! That would not be proper! You may not call upon us until our father returns.

ARLECCHINO (*aside*): Haw – haw!

LELIO: At least, I shall see you again in the loggetta?

ROSAURA (*hopefully*): What think you, sister?

BEATRICE: I think we *may* allow that.

LELIO: And when your father returns, I shall make so bold as to call upon you. Meanwhile—

BEATRICE: We wish your lordship good night. (*Goes into house.*)

ROSAURA (*coquettishly*): Good night – Count Fernando! (*She follows* BEATRICE *into the house.*)

 LELIO *crosses boyishly to* ARLECCHINO, *dropping all his affected swagger.*

LELIO (*down right*): Well, what d'you say to that? I carried it all off quite well, I think!

 He walks front centre, preening himself.

ARLECCHINO: It still beats me how you manage to tell so many lies without getting yourself all mixed up.

LELIO (*turning on him*): Idiot! They are not lies! They're the witty inventions of my fertile mind. (*Going towards the Inn.*) You've got to use your wits, Arlecchino, if you want to enjoy life. (*Turns at the door.*) And make use of your opportunities! (*Goes into the Inn.*)

ARLECCHINO: Make use of your opportunities! Use your wits! He'll have to make good use of *his* wits when his father gets back and finds what a mess his son's got into! Count Fernando! Marquis of Castel d'Oro!

 The light in the loggetta comes up slightly as COLUMBINA *comes out into the loggetta.*

ARLECCHINO (*aside*): Blimey! Another of 'em!

COLUMBINA (*aside – to herself*): Now that my mistresses have gone to bed, I can take a breath of air.

ARLECCHINO (*aside*): Make use of your opportunities, eh? I wonder if this is one?

COLUMBINA (*aside*): Oh, dear, there's a man over there! I think he's looking at me!

ARLECCHINO (*aside*): Well, if *he* can get away with it, I don't see why I shouldn't have a go.

COLUMBINA (*aside*): Oh, dear, I do believe he's going to speak to me!

> ARLECCHINO *comes centre, trying to imitate* LELIO'S *affected 'panache', but sounding like a country yokel, giving his melodramatic interpretation of Romeo.*

ARLECCHINO (*aloud – centre stage*): Oh, what a splendiferous night it is, lit by the beauty of such an incandescent star!

COLUMBINA: Oh, sir – who are you?

ARLECCHINO: I am the Count Obstinato – of Catalania.

COLUMBINA (*aside*): 'Count' is a nobleman's title!

ARLECCHINO: Dare I speak to you, O thou star of delicatiferous beauty?

COLUMBINA: Oh, you needn't be afraid to speak to me, sir. I'm only a poor maidservant.

ARLECCHINO (*aside*): Just my luck! (*Aloud.*) Nevertheless, you are queen of my heart and it is I who am your servant.

COLUMBINA: La, sir! If you go on like that, you will indeed make me conceited.

ARLECCHINO: Ah, but you must believe me. I swear it by all the titles of my nobility.

COLUMBINA: Then I thank you, sir, with all my heart.

ARLECCHINO (*down on his knees to her, with arms outstretched*): Most beautiful one – what would I not do for you?

COLUMBINA (*listening towards house*): Coming! Coming! (*To* ARLECCHINO.) My lord, my ladies are calling me!

ARLECCHINO *staggers to his feet, reaching towards her into the loggetta.*

ARLECCHINO: No! You must not deprive me so soon of the rubiferous shades of your beauty!

COLUMBINA (*drawing back with a squeak*): Oh! Oh, dear, I'm afraid I really can't stay any longer.

ARLECCHINO: We shall meet again?

COLUMBINA: Of course! Good night, my lord. (*Goes into house.*)

ARLECCHINO: Well, I think *I* carried *that* off quite well. There's no doubt about it: if you live with a wolf, you soon learn to howl! (*Goes into the Inn.*)

Carnival music and quick CURTAIN

Scene II

The same. Next morning. FLORINDO *and* BRIGHELLA *come out of the Doctor's house.*

FLORINDO: Listen, Brighella, I have just heard my darling Rosaura tell her sister she would like some silk lace to wear for the Carnival. So I'm going to make her a present of some.

BRIGHELLA: An excellent idea – you can use the occasion to drop a hint about your feelings for her.

FLORINDO: Oh, I'll not let her know it comes from me! Now, don't start that all over again, Brighella; I thought I made things quite clear last night. Here are ten zecchinis. Go and buy about twenty yards of the best silk lace you can find. And tell the merchant to send it to Rosaura, but on no account must he say who it comes from.

BRIGHELLA: Where've you got all this money from?

FLORINDO: Some of it's from my father's allowance and some from my patients' fees.

BRIGHELLA(*going right*): Ay, ay! Easy come, easy go!

FLORINDO: See that the lace is the best!

BRIGHELLA (*as he goes off*): Ten zecchinis!

Left alone, FLORINDO *turns and looks at the balcony.*

FLORINDO (*with sentimental pathos*): There is the dear little loggetta where my sweet one comes. Ah, if she were only to come out there now, I really believe I might have the courage to speak to her. I might *even* say to her . . .

OTTAVIO *enters back right and stands watching* FLORINDO *with amazement.*

FLORINDO: – yes, I *would* say to her: 'Signora, I cannot live without you! You have conquered my heart! Take pity on me, sweet conqueror, and free me from the pangs of unrequited love!'

Turning, he sees OTTAVIO. *Overcoming his embarrassment he quickly pretends to be examining the balcony.*

Ah, Signor Ottavio! I was just admiring the architecture of this little loggetta!

OTTAVIO (*after going over and examining the loggetta minutely*): Yes, it's quite a nice little loggetta, isn't it? But tell me, are you an architect or a portrait painter?

FLORINDO: You know very well I'm studying to be a doctor. What on earth do you mean?

OTTAVIO: I mean – are you intending painting the loggetta by itself – or with the young lady sitting in it?

FLORINDO: I don't know what you're talking about. I'm a doctor, not a painter. Good day to you, Signor Ottavio. (*Tries to pass him.*)

OTTAVIO (*stopping him*): I was only joking, Florindo. After all, we *are* friends, aren't we? So why try to hide the truth from me? I don't hide it from you that I love Beatrice. So, if you love Rosaura, why not tell me? I might be able to help you!

FLORINDO (*haughtily*): I told you I am a doctor and that I was looking at that loggetta merely because I was admiring its design.

OTTAVIO: Have it your own way, then. I don't believe you, of course.

FLORINDO: Well, don't believe me if you don't want to. (*Exit left.*)

OTTAVIO (*looking after him*): He *is* in love! There's no doubt about it. And as he won't tell me anything, I fear it may be Beatrice he admires, and not Rosaura. I must keep my eyes open.

  LELIO *comes out of the Inn.*

LELIO: Why! If it isn't my old friend, Ottavio!

OTTAVIO: Lelio – of all people!

  They shake hands with continental fervour.

LELIO: *You* here – in Venice, Ottavio?

OTTAVIO: And you – you have returned home at last then, Lelio?

LELIO: Yes, I arrived only last night.

OTTAVIO: How on earth did you manage to drag yourself away from Naples? I thought you were completely captivated by the young ladies there?

LELIO (*moving down right*): Aha! Yes! To tell the truth I did have rather a difficult time getting out of their clutches! (*Turning down right*). But do *you* know, though I only arrived in Venice yesterday, I've already made two conquests!

OTTAVIO (*coming forward centre*): No! Ah, well, you always were the lucky one.

LELIO (*in a matter-of-fact tone*): Tell me, Ottavio, do you – er – know Venice well?

OTTAVIO (*moving slightly down left*): Fairly well. I've been staying here for almost a year now.

LELIO (*moving back-centre and looking at the doctor's house*): Do you happen to know – two sisters who – er – live in this house here?

OTTAVIO (*aside, down left*): What's he up to now? (*Aloud.*) Er – no! No, I don't know them.

LELIO (*coming forward centre*): One of them's called Rosaura and the other's called Beatrice. Their father – who's away at present – is a doctor. They're both dazzlingly beautiful girls – and they're both in love with me!

OTTAVIO (*taking step centre*): What! Both of them?

LELIO: Both of them!

OTTAVIO (*another step centre*): But I thought you said you'd only just arrived back in Venice?

LELIO: So I did. And there they were – sitting in that loggetta there – just after I had arrived last night. (*Moving front right.*) As soon as they saw me, they invited me to speak to them.

OTTAVIO (*aside, down left*): Can this be true?

LELIO: No sooner had I spoken a few words, than they were enchanted, and both declared themselves my admirers!

OTTAVIO: *Both* of them?

LELIO (*turning away, right stage, on this line*): Both of them! There wasn't any doubt about it!

OTTAVIO (*aside, down left*): I'm trembling with jealousy.

LELIO (*still speaking out into auditorium, down right*): They invited me into their house!

OTTAVIO (*aside*): I'm trembling all over.

LELIO: I ordered a magnificent supper to be brought in! (*Moving front centre towards* OTTAVIO.) From the Inn, here, of course. And we spent a most hilarious evening, eating and drinking, and – er – drinking and eating!

OTTAVIO (*also moving front centre*): Oh, you're joking! You really can't expect me to believe all this?

LELIO: And why not, pray? What is so incredible about it?

OTTAVIO (*going up to* LELIO): What – you really expect me to believe that two respectable girls, the daughters of a doctor, would take advantage of their father's absence to invite a total stranger into their house and spend the evening drinking with him?

> ARLECCHINO *has come out of the Inn towards the end of this speech and has sauntered down right.*

LELIO: All right! If you don't believe me, here's my servant. Tell me, Arlecchino, what did we do after we had arrived here last night?

ARLECCHINO: Why, sir, we went out for a breath of fresh air.

LELIO: That's right, and didn't I talk to two young ladies in that loggetta?

ARLECCHINO: Aye, that's right, sir, so you did!

LELIO: And then we all had that magnificent meal, didn't we?

ARLECCHINO: Magnifi—?

LELIO (*cutting him short and signing to him to say Yes*): Yes, here, in this house – with the ladies Rosaura and Beatrice.

ARLECCHINO: Oh – yes! (*Laughs loudly and rather artificially*): Yes, of course, sir – with the ladies, sir!

LELIO (*also laughing loudly*): That certainly was a magnificent meal, wasn't it?

ARLECCHINO (*laughing still louder*): *You're* telling *me*, sir!

> LELIO *stops laughing, gives* ARLECCHINO *a reproving look and turns to* OTTAVIO.

LELIO (*to* OTTAVIO): You see? My servant confirms what I was saying in every detail. (ARLECCHINO *saunters back down right again.*)

OTTAVIO: I don't know what to say. You are a very lucky man.

LELIO: Oh, come now, old fellow. I mean to say, it's not all luck, you know.

OTTAVIO: Well, what else can you owe such success to?

LELIO: I don't want to sound boastful, but – well, they've only got to take one look at me, you know, and – bob's your uncle!

OTTAVIO: Oh, I admit you've always got plenty to say for yourself. I had occasion, when we were in Naples together, to be well aware of that. But, really, this does seem too much – even for you. To have two sisters at your feet in one evening!

LELIO (*airily*): My dear fellow, that's nothing to what you're *going* to see!

OTTAVIO: Perhaps. Well, Lelio, I'm afraid that for the moment I must leave you.

LELIO: By the way, where are you staying in Venice?

OTTAVIO (*going towards the Inn*): Here, at this Inn.

LELIO (*aside*): The devil you are! (*Aloud.*) What a coincidence! That is where I am staying – until my father returns to Venice, that is. It's strange I did not see you last night?

OTTAVIO: Oh, I went out to dinner last night and did not return until very late. (*Turns to go into Inn.*)

LELIO: Wait! (OTTAVIO *turns again and* LELIO *goes over to him.*) You've lived here a year, and yet you say you don't know these ladies who live opposite you?

OTTAVIO: Oh, I know them by sight, of course! I merely meant that I have not the honour of their acquaintance.

LELIO: Well, I beg you, do not betray the confidence I have made you. These young ladies might feel offended if they learnt I had discussed them with another.

OTTAVIO (*coldly*): Till our next meeting.

LELIO (*calling after him*): Don't forget! Mum's the word!

OTTAVIO *goes into the Inn.*

ARLECCHINO (*laughing and moving from down right towards centre*): That was a close shave!

LELIO (*coming forward, down right*): I don't see what is so funny about it.

ARLECCHINO (*returning to him, down right*): Why, I knew all the time that that gentleman was staying at the Inn!

LELIO: Then why couldn't you have tipped me the wink, you fool?

ARLECCHINO: Look, master, how *can* I tip you the wink, when I don't know from one minute to the next when you're going to tell one of your lies?

LELIO: How many times have I got to tell you, they're *not* lies? They're witty inventions!

ARLECCHINO: Well, look, sir – when you're going to make one of your – witty inventions – *you* tip *me* the wink – give me some sort of signal – and then I'll be all ready to back you up.

LELIO: I don't see why you find it so difficult. You're usually quite quick on the up-take.

ARLECCHINO: It's just that your lies – beg your pardon, sir – your witty inventions, come so sudden-like, I get all flummoxed. I'll tell you what, sir – you pretend to have caught a bit of a cold and give a little sneeze-like and I'll know that that's the signal for me to back you up.

ROSAURA *and* COLUMBINA *come out of their house, holding small black masks before their faces.*

LELIO (*aside*): Well, now's your opportunity. Here they are now, so don't let me down this time.

ARLECCHINO (*aside, in a loud whisper*): What have they got their faces covered for?

LELIO (*aside*): It's Carnival time! Ladies always wear masks here when they go out during Carnival time. (*He crosses* ARLECCHINO *and goes towards the girls*.)

ARLECCHINO (*aside*): Sounds a daft idea to me.

LELIO (*approaching* ROSAURA *and* COLUMBINA *who have been standing talking outside their door*): Ladies, though you may hide your faces, your beauty, shining from your eyes, still betrays your identities.

ROSAURA: This, my lord, is *not* my sister. It is my maid.

ARLECCHINO (*aside*): My bit of stuff, eh?

LELIO (*quickly, to cover his mistake*): Why, then I may indeed speak freely, and tell you that it is you only who inspires my entire devotion.

ROSAURA: So, my lord, you *can* distinguish me from my sister, though not my sister from my maid?

LELIO: Of course! My love would in truth be worth but little, if I did not know you even when masked.

ROSAURA: How *do* you know me, pray?

LELIO: By your voice, your eyes, your queenly air – and by my heart – which is ignorant of the art of lying.

ROSAURA: Tell me, then, who am I?

LELIO: You – are the queen of my heart!

ROSAURA: Quite so! But *what* is my *name*?

ARLECCHINO (*aside*): Go on – have a go!

LELIO (*having a go*): Rosaura!

ROSAURA: Bravo! (*She lowers her mask.*) Now I see you really know me. It all really *is* true!

LELIO: I, Count Fernando, Marquis of Castel d'Oro, cannot lie. For nearly a whole year I have been your most humble admirer. (*To* ARLECCHINO.) Isn't that true?

> *He takes out his handkerchief and sneezes into it.* ARLEC-
> CHINO, *however, does not notice since he is gazing soulfully at*
> COLUMBINA – *who is affecting to be disdainfully uninterested.*
> LELIO *takes in the situation and turns back to* ROSAURA.

LELIO (*to* ROSAURA): Please excuse me, I seem to have caught a slight chill. (*He strides right to* ARLECCHINO *and pushes him.*)

LELIO (*to* ARLECCHINO): Answer me! That's true, isn't it?

ARLECCHINO (*coming back to reality*): Oh, yes, *yes*, sir. That's quite true.

ROSAURA: But why couldn't you have declared yourself before this, my lord?

LELIO: I will tell you. A year ago I left Naples, rather than be forced by my father into a marriage which was hateful to me. Naturally it has not been easy to persuade my father to accept the choice I have made myself. It was only yesterday that I received his letter of consent.

ROSAURA: Your father really has consented to your marrying a doctor's daughter?

LELIO: I have received his whole-hearted blessing.

He glances at ARLECCHINO *and sees that he is still gazing soulfully across at* COLUMBINA *down left.*

LELIO (*to* ROSAURA): Excuse me.

He goes up to ARLECCHINO *right, and sneezes loudly.* ARLECCHINO *jumps.*

ARLECCHINO: Ay, that's true! I read the letter myself.

ROSAURA: But my dowry! *My* father can hardly afford the dowry expected by a man of your position, my lord.

LELIO: The House of Castel d'Oro has no need of dowries!

ROSAURA: You really aren't just amusing yourself at my expense, are you, my lord?

LELIO: Surely, my sweet, you do not doubt my word? Why, even as a child, I was incapable of telling a lie. (ARLECCHINO *shakes with silent laughter.*) You've only to ask my servant here. (*He sneezes loudly.*)

ARLECCHINO (*pulling himself together*): Oh, yes, signora, you

can rely on my master (*aside*) – to tell the biggest whoppers
you ever heard.

ROSAURA: When may I hope to see some proof then, my
lord, of your feelings for me?

LELIO: The moment your father returns to Venice.

ROSAURA: Yes, that will indeed test the sincerity of your
feelings.

LELIO: Your father, my sweet one, will find no sincerer
man than I in all Venice.

> *A Draper's* BOY *enters back right, carrying a box.* ROSAURA
> *puts on her mask again. The* BOY *knocks at the* DOCTOR'S
> *door.*

ROSAURA: Whom do you want, young man?

BOY: Is this the house of Doctor Balanzoni?

ROSAURA: Certainly. Who are you looking for?

BOY: I have to deliver this box to Signora Rosaura, the
Doctor's daughter.

ROSAURA: I am she. What is in the box? Who sent it?

BOY: It's twenty yards of silk lace. My master told me to
deliver them to you. We don't know the name of the person
who ordered it.

ROSAURA: In that case, you can take it back again. I don't
receive presents without knowing who they come from.

BOY: But it's paid for! It cost ten zecchinis!

ROSAURA: I don't care how much it cost. I've told you I
won't receive it.

LELIO (*moving centre*): Signora Rosaura, may I say how much
I admire your delicacy? And, as you refuse to take them
without knowing who they come from, I am forced to tell
you that it was I who ordered them.

ARLECCHINO (*aside*): Well, can you beat that!

ROSAURA: You? It is a present from you? But why did you
not wish me to know?

LELIO: Because I was ashamed to offer you so trivial a thing.

BOY (*coming forward right centre*): Sir, I'll have you know you'll not find better lace in all Venice.

LELIO: Probably. But I have always been a difficult person to please.

ARLECCHINO (*aside*): What a lad he is!

ROSAURA: In that case, I shall be very pleased to accept them, my lord. As a matter of fact, I was only saying to my sister today how much I should like some new lace for my Carnival dress. Take them into the house, Columbina, and tomorrow you shall arrange them on my dress.

> ARLECCHINO *gazes despairingly at* COLUMBINA *as she takes the box and goes into the house.*

ROSAURA: With your permission, my lord, I also will go in now. I really only came out to see whether it was me whom you favoured!

LELIO (*escorting her to the door*): My heart goes with you, light of my life.

ROSAURA (*turning*): But wait – what am I to say to my sister?

LELIO: My sweet one, I would rather she did not know for the time being of our understanding. Let us keep it a secret – until I have seen your father?

ROSAURA: Yes, perhaps that will be best. (*Goes into the house.*)

BOY (*to* LELIO): Is there anything else you desire, sir?

LELIO: No, you may go.

BOY: Oh, *sir*, what about the tip?

LELIO: I'll be seeing you later.

BOY: Yes – not if you can help it, I bet. (*Goes right.*)

LELIO (*to* ARLECCHINO, *who appears fed-up*): Well, what did you think of her? A beauty, isn't she?

ARLECCHINO: Why couldn't she have taken that thing off her face?

LELIO: I'm not talking about the maid! What did you think of Rosaura? Isn't she just a masterpiece of charms?

ARLECCHINO (*drily*): Aye, and your Honour's a masterpiece of witty inventions.

LELIO (*crossing front stage to down left*): She seems, though, to have some secret admirer. He must be too shy to come out into the open. Well, it is his own fault if other people profit from it.

 COLUMBINA *comes out of the house again.* ARLECCHINO *moves quickly across to* LELIO.

ARLECCHINO (*aside to* LELIO): Back me up, master. (*Aloud, to* COLUMBINA, *who is crossing to Inn door.*) Young lady, if I am not mistaken, it was you I spoke with last night?

COLUMBINA (*turning at Inn door and lowering her mask*): *You* are Don Obstinato?

ARLECCHINO: At your service.

COLUMBINA (*coming forward right centre*): I can't believe it. You're not dressed like a nobleman.

ARLECCHINO: But I *am* a nobleman, *very* noble – *and* very rich. If you don't believe me, ask my friend here. (*He sneezes towards* LELIO.)

COLUMBINA: Bless you![1]

ARLECCHINO (*to* COLUMBINA): Don't mention it! (*He gazes reproachfully at* LELIO, *who is affecting a complete lack of interest.*)

COLUMBINA: But if you are both so noble and so rich, why are you travelling without any servants?

ARLECCHINO: Well, you see, as a matter of fact, the Duke of Sorrento – a great friend of ours – wagered us a thousand zecchinis that we couldn't travel to Venice and back with-

[1] The terrible plagues which occurred in Italy began with fits of sneezing and yawning. Pope Gregory VII decreed that 'God bless you' should be said to those who sneezed, and that the sign of the Cross be made over those who yawned.

out any of our servants. (*He sneezes again towards* LELIO.)

COLUMBINA: Bless you!

ARLECCHINO (*to* COLUMBINA): Don't mention it! It's the tobacco. Tickles my nose. (*Aside to* LELIO.) Master – I sneezed!

LELIO (*aside to* ARLECCHINO): I can't wait about here all day.

COLUMBINA: Where are you from, sir?

ARLECCHINO: I come from the great city of Rome, where I am related to all the noble families. (*He sneezes loudly.*)

COLUMBINA: Bless you!

ARLECCHINO (*to* COLUMBINA): Don't mention it! (*Aside to* LELIO.) Why don't you back me up?

LELIO (*aside to* ARLECCHINO): You lay it on too thick!

COLUMBINA: Your friend there, the lord marquis, has made my lady a fine present.

ARLECCHINO: And I will give you an even better one. You just go to the shops and order what you like – I'll pay. You just get what you like – anything up to, say, half a million zecchinis.

COLUMBINA: That does it! Now I know you're having me on. (*Goes back into house, slamming the door after her.*)

LELIO: I told you, didn't I? You just don't know how to go about it. You go too far.

ARLECCHINO: But I thought the bigger you tell 'em, the more they'll believe 'em.

LELIO: I'm going in to find Ottavio. I must tell him of my latest adventure. (*Goes into the Inn.*)

ARLECCHINO: Here we go again. More witty inventions. I'd better watch more carefully how he does it. (*Follows* LELIO *into the Inn.*)

    PANTALONE *and* DOCTOR BALANZONI *enter left, followed by two* PORTERS *carrying their trunks. The*

PORTERS, *without being told, take the trunks one into* PANTALONE'S *house and the other into the* DOCTOR'S *house, and then go off again left.*

DOCTOR: Thanks be to heaven, we have arrived back safely.

PANTALONE: We've certainly arrived back – and quicker than we went.

DOCTOR: And it certainly has been a most profitable journey for *me*. The patient I treated in Padua paid me ten zecchinis; I have had a very pleasant stay at your country villa; and best of all we have arranged the marriage between your son, Lelio, and my daughter, Rosaura!

PANTALONE: My dear doctor, you have no idea how much it pleases me that, after being friends for so many years, we are now to become related to each other through the marriage of our children.

DOCTOR: Let me shake you by the hand. (*Emotionally.*) Ay ay! Two old friends – and soon we'll be having the same grandchildren. (*They both take out their handkerchiefs and wipe their eyes, with great emotion. Whilst they are doing so, the* COACH DRIVER *comes on back right and goes into the Inn.*) When did you say your son would be arriving in Venice?

PANTALONE: His last letter said he was about to leave Rome. He should be here today or tomorrow.

DOCTOR: And to think that you may not even recognize him!

PANTALONE: You must remember he was still only a boy when his mother died and I decided it would be best for him to go to his aunt and uncle in Naples. Now he has learnt his uncle's business and they tell me he has indeed become a fine young gentleman.

DOCTOR: You make me more determined than ever that Rosaura shall marry him. To tell you the truth, old friend, I had thought of marrying her to my pupil, Florindo. He comes from an excellent family in Bologna. But that young fellow seems to be a confirmed woman-hater. And so, I decided to discuss the matter with you – with these most happy results. Yes, yes, I must go in and tell my daughters all about it.

> *He goes into his house. As* PANTALONE *is going towards his door, an uproar is heard within the Inn.* PANTALONE *stops and turns, back-stage, as out of the Inn, backwards and shaking his fist, comes the angry* COACH DRIVER *followed by* LELIO.

COACH DRIVER: Call yourself a gentleman! I wonder you're not ashamed giving me such a miserly little tip after driving you all the way from Naples!

> PANTALONE *moves slowly forward again front left, watching them.*

LELIO (*disdainfully*): Tips, you insolent fellow, are optional, not obligatory!

COACH DRIVER: You keep that sort of language for them that appreciates it. All I know is, that I should have had at least three zecchinis for driving you all the way from Naples.

PANTALONE (*aside, down left*): From Naples! Perhaps he knows my son!

LELIO: Oh, go away! And don't make so much noise!

COACH DRIVER: I should have known better. They're all the same, these so-called gentlemen. (*Goes right.*)

LELIO (*calling after him*): Take care, or I'll come after you and give you a good beating! (*Aside.*) Perhaps I'd better not, though.

PANTALONE (*aside*): This might even *be* my son!

LELIO (*still back-stage, looking off*): They're all the same – these coachmen! Always out to do you, if they can.

PANTALONE (*aside*): I'd better be careful. I'd look a fool if it

isn't him. (*Aloud, as* LELIO *goes towards Inn door.*) Excuse
me, your Honour, but have you just come from Naples?

LELIO: Why, yes, sir.

PANTALONE: Really, now! I have quite a number of cus-
tomers in Naples. Perhaps your Honour might even be one
of them?

LELIO: I am the Count of Ancona, sir, at your service.

PANTALONE (*aside*): It's not him after all! (*Aloud.*) Perhaps,
your Honour may have met a certain Lelio Bisognosi in
Naples?

LELIO: Lelio Bisognosi! Why, sir, I know him well! A great
friend of mine, sir. A most excellent young man, full of wit,
liked by everyone. All the young ladies are always running
after him. Yes, indeed, sir, he is quite the idol of all Naples.
And what's more, sir, a most honest and upright young
man, absolutely incapable of uttering an untruth.

PANTALONE: Oh, your Honour, you have no idea how glad
I am to hear you speak so highly of him! (*Takes out his
handkerchief.*) Ay, ay! It nigh makes me cry with happiness!

OTTAVIO *comes out of the Inn.*

OTTAVIO: Well, congratulations, Signor Pantalone, on your
good fortune!

PANTALONE: What good fortune, Signor Ottavio?

OTTAVIO: Why, the return of your son, of course.

PANTALONE: He's come? Lelio's here? Oh, I must go in
and welcome him. (*Starts going towards his door.*)

LELIO (*aside*): My father! That's torn it!

OTTAVIO (*calling after* PANTALONE): But he's here! Weren't
you just speaking to him?

PANTALONE (*turning slowly*): Signor – the Count – of Ancona!

LELIO (*laughing artificially*): Ha, ha, ha! Dear old father, still
always ready for a joke, eh? But you do forgive me,
don't you? You see, *I* knew you at once, and I just couldn't

help having a bit of a joke. Please, please, forgive me.

PANTALONE: Of course, of course I do, my dear boy. But you shouldn't tell lies, even for a joke, you know.

LELIO: I know, Father. It won't happen again, I promise you.

PANTALONE: Well, let me have a good look at you, lad. Ay, ay! What a fine gentleman you've grown into! No wonder I didn't know you. But let's not stand here talking. Come into the house, lad. You'll excuse us, Signor Ottavio.

OTTAVIO: Your servant, sir.

PANTALONE (*as he goes towards his door*): Ay ay! What a fine young man he is. A real gentleman he's become!

LELIO (*aside to* OTTAVIO): Rosaura and Beatrice both came out to look for me this morning! This is in confidence. Keep it to yourself!

Follows PANTALONE *into his house.*

OTTAVIO (*moving down right*): I just can't get over the behaviour of those two girls. I should never have thought they would take advantage of their father's absence like this.

The DOCTOR *comes out of his house and comes centre.*

DOCTOR : Your servant, Signor Ottavio.

OTTAVIO (*bowing*): Your servant, my dear Doctor. I rejoice to see that you have returned home safely.

DOCTOR: I have returned, sir, to an empty house, it appears. (*He goes back stage and looks off right, then returns centre.*) My daughters, I find, are both not at home. Perhaps you have seen them go out, Signor Ottavio?

OTTAVIO: I regret, sir, that I have not had that pleasure. (*Aside, as the* DOCTOR *goes down left and looks off.*) Poor old chap, much credit his daughters will do him. By refusing me Beatrice, he's certainly saved me from making a bad match.

The DOCTOR *becomes aware of* OTTAVIO'S *continued presence and silence.*

DOCTOR (*aside, down left*): He's sulking because I've kept refusing him Beatrice. I'll try to put things right. (*Aloud.*) Signor Ottavio. I have news for you. My daughter Rosaura is to be married.

OTTAVIO (*coldly*): I am delighted to hear it, sir.

DOCTOR: So now I've only Beatrice to get settled.

OTTAVIO (*meaningfully*): That should not be difficult.

DOCTOR: Ha, ha! I understand your meaning, Signor Ottavio. Yes indeed, I have decided at last to give her to you. Beatrice is yours, Signor Ottavio.

OTTAVIO (*unconcernedly*): Thanks awfully, but I'm afraid I'm no longer interested.

DOCTOR: What d'ye mean, sir? Are you trying to get your own back for my previous refusals?

OTTAVIO: You may marry her to whom you will, sir. *I* am no longer interested.

DOCTOR (*shaking his stick angrily*): Explain yourself, sir. Why this sudden change of heart?

OTTAVIO: Perhaps I should not say this, sir, but the respect I bear for you forces me to. There is no change of heart. My feelings for Beatrice are still the same, but I would that they were not. I am compelled to act as I do, even though *you* are blind to what is going on about you.

DOCTOR: Have you taken leave of your senses, sir? What on earth are you talking about?

OTTAVIO: Sir, last night, your two daughters admitted a stranger into your house and spent the evening eating and drinking with him.

DOCTOR: Ridiculous, sir! (*He thumps his stick and stumps down left.*)

OTTAVIO: I can prove it, sir!

DOCTOR: You shall, sir! By gad, sir, you certainly *shall* prove it.

OTTAVIO: More than that, sir. The very man who was admitted to your house shall prove it to you. I shall bring him to you before the day is out, and you shall hear it from his own lips. (*Goes into the Inn.*)

DOCTOR: It can't be true! It's just not possible. But I must find out. Oh, no, such a thing could never happen to me. But how can I find out?

FLORINDO *enters left.*

DOCTOR: Ah, Florindo! Florindo, my boy, a word with you, if you please. Tell me – and on your honour tell me the truth – did my daughters admit a strange young man to my house yesterday evening?

FLORINDO: Upon my honour, Doctor, no one at all came into your house last night. Whatever gave you that idea?

DOCTOR: You know Signor Ottavio?

FLORINDO: Of course.

DOCTOR: He told me that a strange young man had supper with my daughters in my house – and he says he can prove it.

FLORINDO: Then he is either lying or has been grossly deceived by someone.

DOCTOR: Oh, my dear boy, how relieved I am to hear you say this. My daughters are both out – or I would have demanded an explanation from them.

He looks off stage.

DOCTOR: Ah, but here is Rosaura, now.

FLORINDO (*stammering*): Sir, I – I have work to do. If you will excuse me. (*He dashes into the* DOCTOR'S *house.*)

ROSAURA *and* COLUMBINA *enter left.*

ROSAURA: Dear Father, you have returned! Oh, how glad I am to see you!

DOCTOR: And I to see you, my daughter! Especially after what I have just heard about you and your sister, that you both actually forgot yourselves so far as to entertain a stranger to supper last night.

ROSAURA: Father!

DOCTOR: Calm yourself, my child. I have been assured that it has all been invented by somebody, though for what purpose I cannot imagine.

ROSAURA: But who could have made up such a monstrous lie?

DOCTOR: As a matter of fact, it was Ottavio who told me about it. He actually had the nerve to say that he could prove it. I shall certainly demand an explanation when I see him.

COLUMBINA: I'll go and see if he is in the Inn, shall I?

DOCTOR: Do, and if he's there, say I want to speak to him at once.

COLUMBINA: I'll see he comes – whether he wants to or not! (*Goes into the Inn.*)

DOCTOR (*moving right centre*): All this has made me forget the most happy news I have for you, my child.

ROSAURA: For me, Father?

DOCTOR: Rosaura, my dear daughter, I have promised your hand in marriage to the son of my dear old friend, Signor Pantalone.

ROSAURA (*moving forward left centre*): Oh, no, Father, if you love me, *no*!

DOCTOR (*returning centre*): But surely you've always wanted a good marriage arranged for you?

ROSAURA: I must tell you, Father, that a great nobleman wishes to marry me.

DOCTOR (*going to her, left centre*): What great nobleman?

ROSAURA: I have only spoken twice with him, but he has

admired me from a distance for nearly a year now. He said he will present himself to you on your return.

DOCTOR (*moving across slowly right*): My dear child! If this is true I most certainly shall not stand in your way. (*Aside, down right.*) I can soon find some excuse to make to Pantalone. (*Returning centre stage.*) But what is this great nobleman's name?

> BEATRICE *enters back right, unnoticed by them, and stands listening.*

ROSAURA: The Marquis Fernando of Castel d'Oro.

DOCTOR: A marquis! Great heavens! (*Goes to her, left.*) You're quite certain his intentions are serious?

ROSAURA: He has given me his word!

DOCTOR (*returning centre*): Good gracious, I must certainly do my best to help you, if that's the way things are.

BEATRICE (*coming forward, right stage*): You let yourself be taken in too easily, Father. Don Fernando has only told us that he admires one of us. He has not told us which. I have every reason to believe, however, that it is me he prefers.

DOCTOR (*turning to* ROSAURA, *on his left*): What *is* all this?

ROSAURA (*speaking across to* BEATRICE, *right*): What makes you think it is you he prefers?

BEATRICE (*speaking across* DOCTOR *to* ROSAURA, *left*): What makes *you* think he prefers you?

ROSAURA (*to* DOCTOR): Father, *I* know what I am speaking about.

BEATRICE (*to* DOCTOR): And so do I.

> As the DOCTOR *bellows at them, shaking his stick, they both retreat quickly and stand looking sullenly in front of them,* BEATRICE *right stage and* ROSAURA, *left.*

DOCTOR: Be quiet, both of you! It seems to me you've got yourselves into a fine mix-up. You'll both stay in the house and not go out without my permission. If this Lord

Marquis does speak to me, I'll soon find out which of you is the favoured one. But if you ask me, you're both so set on finding yourselves husbands that you're both going daft about it.

He goes bad-temperedly into his house. ROSAURA *glances over her shoulder to make sure he has gone before she speaks.*

ROSAURA (*to* BEATRICE): *When* did he say he preferred you?

BEATRICE: Well, when did he ever say he preferred *you*?

ROSAURA (*moving down left*): After all, I am the elder sister, and I do think . . .

BEATRICE: Yes, if it weren't for you, I could have been married fifty times. (*Tosses her head superciliously.*)

ROSAURA (*turning on her, sarcastically*): Who to? Signor Ottavio? Do you know your precious Ottavio has been inventing a lot of stories about us entertaining strangers whilst our father was away?

BEATRICE (*moving right centre*): Ottavio!

ROSAURA (*moving left centre*): Father has just been telling me about it.

BEATRICE: Why, the ungrateful wretch!

COLUMBINA *and* OTTAVIO *come out of the Inn.*

COLUMBINA: Here is Signor Ottavio, my ladies.

She stands back left. OTTAVIO *comes centre.*

ROSAURA (*going to one side of him*): You despicable liar!

BEATRICE (*going to the other side of him*): You infamous deceiver!

OTTAVIO: OH! I'M NOT!!

ROSAURA: Who told my father that we had entertained a strange young man in our house?

OTTAVIO: I did, but . . .

ROSAURA: Then – you're a liar!

BEATRICE: And a deceiver!

OTTAVIO: Please *listen*! You know Lelio—

ROSAURA: Did you – or did you not – say we had entertained a stranger?

OTTAVIO: Yes, but only because . . .

ROSAURA: Liar! (*She goes into house.*)

BEATRICE: Base deceiver! (*She follows.*)

OTTAVIO: But they won't let me speak! Columbina, you must make them listen to me. I've got to tell them the truth!

COLUMBINA (*coming left of him*): That you *didn't* say that they had been entertaining a strange young man?

OTTAVIO: Well – yes – I *said* it – but you see—

COLUMBINA: Then they were right. You are a deceiver and a liar! (*She goes into the house.*)

OTTAVIO: Oh, this is too much! Even their maid insults me! How on earth can I put things right? *And* what on earth will their father say? If only I had spoken to Florindo before I'd told their father what Lelio said to me. It's Lelio who's the liar! Oh, lord, here's their father now!

  The DOCTOR *erupts from his house.*

DOCTOR: Ah! They told me you were here!

OTTAVIO: Sir, I am grovelling at your feet! Florindo has told me all.

DOCTOR: And so you should be, sir! To tell me such a pack of lies, sir!

OTTAVIO: Sir, my only excuse is that I had every reason to believe in the reliability of the person who told me.

DOCTOR: And, pray, who was this person?

OTTAVIO: Why, Lelio, of course. Lelio Bisognosi.

DOCTOR: Signor Pantalone's son?

OTTAVIO: Yes.

DOCTOR: Then he *has* arrived in Venice?

OTTAVIO: He arrived yesterday – worse luck for me.

DOCTOR: But *why* should *he* make up such a ridiculous story about my daughters? Does he *know* that Rosaura and Beatrice *are* my daughters?

OTTAVIO: I think so. He certainly knows that they are the daughters of a doctor.

DOCTOR (*turning left, thumping his stick*): Well, one thing's certain, he won't marry Rosaura after this!

OTTAVIO (*going right of him*): And – er – the Signora Beatrice? You will not hold all this unfortunate misunderstanding against me, sir?

DOCTOR: I cannot help remembering that you refused her not an hour ago.

OTTAVIO: At least, sir, you will allow me to call upon her, to make my apologies.

DOCTOR: Yes, you may do that.

OTTAVIO: Thank you, sir. I am indeed your most grateful servant, sir. (*Bows.*) I shall have the honour of waiting upon the Signora Beatrice this evening.

He goes into the Inn.

DOCTOR: So! This is the sort of son Pantalone has, is it? And to think I agreed only yesterday to his marriage to Rosaura. Well, if this young Marquis does indeed ask for Rosaura's hand, Pantalone will certainly not be able to blame me after this, if I break the marriage agreement I made with him yesterday. Perhaps, I'd better try and avoid seeing Pantalone, until I've managed to speak with this young Marquis – oh, dear, what did they say his name was? He might even be lodging somewhere quite close by! (*Looks around.*)

ARLECCHINO *comes out of the Inn, looking for* LELIO.

DOCTOR: Ah, you! Come here a moment, fellow!

ARLECCHINO (*strutting haughtily right centre*): I beg your pardon! You cannot be aware who you are addressing of. I happen to be the Count Obstinato of Catalonia.

DOCTOR (*going right of him obsequiously*): I beg *your* pardon, sir!

I had no idea! Your dress, sir, misled me – no doubt you are attired thus for the Carnival. My humble apologies for addressing you so, sir.

ARLECCHINO (*swaggering down right*): Granted, I'm sure. Yes, as a matter of fact, I'm staying at this 'ere Inn with my friend the Marquis of Castel d'Oro.

DOCTOR (*who has been going towards his door but now turns quickly*): Who did you say?

ARLECCHINO: My friend, the Marquis of Castel d'Oro!

DOCTOR (*coming centre*): That's it! *That* was the name! He's staying at this Inn, you say?

ARLECCHINO: That is correct. We both, he and I, are staying, for the moment, at this Inn.

DOCTOR: Oh, would you oblige me, sir, by telling your friend, the Marquis, that I shall have the great honour of calling upon him this afternoon? I am Doctor Balanzoni. It is a matter of great importance that I should speak with the Marquis as soon as possible. (*Goes towards the house.*) It was indeed fortunate, our meeting like this. Until this afternoon, then. (*Goes into house.*)

ARLECCHINO (*looks at closed door thoughtfully*): I don't like the sound of this. *If* that chap's *a doctor*, and if he lives in *that* house, and *if* he wants to see the *Marquis of Castel d'Oro* so urgently – it looks as though my master's going to have to think up some very witty inventions very quick indeed.

QUICK CURTAIN

ACT II

Scene I

Afternoon of the same day. ARLECCHINO *is pacing up and down outside the Inn, still waiting for* LELIO.

ARLECCHINO: I'm just about fed-up hanging around waiting for this master of mine. He's been gone about three hours now and here am I without any money – and they won't even serve me a meal at the Inn until he comes back. Where on earth can he have got to? Gone off paying visits, I suppose. Never gives a thought to his poor servant, waiting here for him – starving.

    LELIO *comes out of his father's house.*

ARLECCHINO: So there you are! Where've you been to all this time?

LELIO: My father's back! I've just come out to tell you to fetch my trunk over from the Inn.

ARLECCHINO: Do *you* know I've had no dinner?

LELIO: Never mind that now. Go and do as I say and then you'll eat.

ARLECCHINO (*going towards the Inn*): Well, I hope your father's got a good cook; I'm fair famished. (*Turns at the Inn door.*) Oh, by the way, there's been somebody looking for you – says he wants to have an urgent word with you.

LELIO: Who was it?

ARLECCHINO (*coming centre again*): The father of them two girls you've been leading up the garden path.

LELIO: Good heavens! What did you tell him?

ARLECCHINO: I'd already told him you were the Marquis of Castel d'Oro before I knew who he was. He said he'd wait on you this afternoon at the Inn.

LELIO: Quickly, let's get the trunk over into the house before he turns up! Oh, heavens, here's my father now!

PANTALONE *comes out of the house.*

ARLECCHINO (*aside, going down right*): Wow! What a beard!

PANTALONE (*coming left of* LELIO): You seemed a long time, my boy! I can't bear to let you out of my sight.

LELIO: I'm sorry, Father, but this servant of mine never hurries himself.

ARLECCHINO (*speaking across to* PANTALONE): Signor Pantalone, it goes without saying, that being the humble servant of your youthful prodigy here (*indicates* LELIO), I allow myself the prodigious honour of protesting myself also your honour's most humble and obedient servant.

PANTALONE (*to* LELIO): What a charming speech. (*In a loud aside.*) But a bit of a fool, eh?

ARLECCHINO (*overhearing him – aside*): It takes a fool to know a fool. (*Aloud.*) Yes, sir, I plays the fool to order!

PANTALONE: Excellent! Excellent! There's nothing I like better than a good laugh. You will come in very useful.

ARLECCHINO: You won't forget, though, sir, will you, that fools eat a lot more than ordinary folk?

PANTALONE: I'll see you don't go empty! You have my word for it.

ARLECCHINO: I'd rather like to see, now, if you're a man of your word!

PANTALONE: All right – you can go down to the kitchen

and help yourself – but make sure you don't forget my son's trunk from the Inn afterwards.

ARLECCHINO: Now, there speaks a man of his *word*, right enough. (*Aside to* LELIO, *as he passes him.*) You *sure* he's your father? (*Goes into* PANTALONE'S *house.*)

LELIO (*aside*): That fellow's getting above himself.

PANTALONE: He seems quite a card, that servant of yours. But now, whilst we're alone, I really must tell you what I've been arranging for you.

LELIO: Arranging for me?

PANTALONE: Ay, lad. It's time you married and settled down. Well, it's all arranged: a good wife, a good dowry! What more could you want?

LELIO: But who? Who is she? Aren't I even allowed to see her first?

PANTALONE (*moving pompously down left*): There's a proper way of doing these things and you'll see her when you sign the marriage contract and not before. You can trust me; I've done well for you, lad.

LELIO (*aside, down right*): It's time for a witty invention!

PANTALONE: What's that?

LELIO (*crossing to him down left*): Father, I cannot keep my secret from you any longer.

PANTALONE: What secret? What *are* you talking about!

LELIO (*kneeling*): I throw myself at your feet.

PANTALONE: What is it? What've you been up to!

LELIO: I can hardly dare tell you.

PANTALONE: Oh, get up! For heaven's sake, out with it, boy!

LELIO (*rising and turning front before speaking*): I am already married, Father. I have a wife in Naples.

PANTALONE: What! You – you tell me this *now*! Why wasn't I told before? Does your uncle know?

LELIO (*moving away front centre, obviously inventing furiously*):

No – my uncle – does not know. He – he was dangerously ill when it happened.

PANTALONE: But why couldn't you have written and told me? Why couldn't you have brought the girl with you?

LELIO (*moving further front right, extemporizing madly*): I – I wanted to tell you all about it myself first.

PANTALONE (*speaking slowly, obviously reflecting that his son is still 'a fine young gentleman'*): Well – if it's done – it's done. I can only hope you've shown some sense, and not chosen some common hussy.

LELIO (*down right*): Father! She is a most respectable lady. A nobleman's daughter, as well.

PANTALONE (*taking a step left, showing cautious interest*): Of Naples?

LELIO: Yes – and the dowry is more than you could ever have dreamed of.

PANTALONE (*moving front centre, now obviously interested*): Her father's a nobleman – *and* very wealthy, eh?

LELIO: Oh, extremely wealthy!

PANTALONE (*moving right centre, becoming pompously jocular again*): Well, well, and what is the young lady's name?

LELIO: Briseide.

PANTALONE (*now down right, beside* LELIO): And her father?

LELIO: He is Don Policarpio of Albacava.

PANTALONE (*turning away centre, with fond reproval*): He must think you've got a fine father – not having written him a line about all this. I'd better go in and write to him now. (*Turning, front centre.*) What did you say his name was?

LELIO: Don Policarpio of Abacabage.

PANTALONE: Have a cabbage? What – what sort of name is that?

LELIO: Well – you see—

PANTALONE: *Now*, I remember – you said Don Policarpio of Albacava.

LELIO: Yes, that's right – you see, Abacabage is his feudal title – sometimes he uses one and sometimes the other.

PANTALONE: I see! Well, I must go in and write to him and tell him to send this daughter-in-law of mine along to visit me. I'll just be in time to catch the Naples post. (*Goes into house.*)

LELIO: I'll have to work fast. Nobody's going to marry me off to any girl but Rosaura. Once I'm married to her, my Neapolitan wife can suddenly become a Venetian one.

Exit back right.

BRIGHELLA enters left and is about to open the door of the DOCTOR'S house, when it opens and FLORINDO comes out.

FLORINDO: Oh, Brighella, thank heaven I've found you! I'm quite desperate!

BRIGHELLA: Now what's gone wrong?

FLORINDO: Doctor Balanzoni is going to marry Rosaura to a Neapolitan Marquis!

BRIGHELLA: Who told you that?

FLORINDO: Her sister, Beatrice.

BRIGHELLA: Then you've no time to lose – you've just got to declare yourself.

FLORINDO: Yes, Brighella, that's exactly what I'm going to do. (*Goes forward, left centre.*) That is why I have written *this poem*!

BRIGHELLA: *Poem!* What good'll that do?

FLORINDO: It will reveal everything to Rosaura! Look! Isn't the handwriting beautiful?

BRIGHELLA: But that's not *your* handwriting!

FLORINDO: Of course not. I've had it copied out.

BRIGHELLA: What on earth for?

FLORINDO: Because she *knows my* handwriting!

BRIGHELLA: I don't get it. Isn't she supposed to *know* it's from you?

FLORINDO: Listen! And then tell me whether you don't think this speaks clearly enough. (*Reads.*)

> 'Queen of my heart, goddess divine,
>   For love of you, Rosaura mine,
>   In silence I suffer and pine.
> No lord am I, no proud titles mine;
>   My profession is my only sign
>   Of rank or wealth, Rosaura mine.
> Oh, how often you see me near you,
>   Sorrowful and silent, yet true!
> Only for your sake I in Venice live
>   Far, far from Lombardy whence I came.
> Thus to you do I reveal my love.
> Soon to you will I reveal my name.'

There! What d'you think of that?

BRIGHELLA: I don't see how she'll be any the wiser when she's read that.

FLORINDO: Why not? Every line plainly indicates that it was I who wrote it.

BRIGHELLA: Well, I suppose if *you* give it her yourself, she *may* guess it was you that wrote it.

FLORINDO: Oh, no, I'm not giving it her myself.

BRIGHELLA (*with forced patience*): What *are* you going to do then?

FLORINDO: Well, I had thought of throwing it into the loggetta there.

BRIGHELLA: But suppose somebody else finds it?

FLORINDO: Whoever finds it will see it's addressed to Rosaura, and they'll give it to her.

BRIGHELLA: *I* think it would be better—

FLORINDO: No! I'm going to do it my way! (*He throws the poem into the loggetta.*) Quick! I think somebody's coming!

BRIGHELLA: Let's wait and see what happens!

FLORINDO: No, no! Come on! Quickly! (*Exit back right.*)

BRIGHELLA (*following him*): You ain't the lad your father was – *that* you ain't! (*Exit left, after him, back right.*)

   COLUMBINA *comes out on to the Balcony.*

COLUMBINA (*as she sees the paper*): Yes, I *thought* something fell into the loggetta. It's a piece of paper. (*Picks it up and opens it.*) Oh, it's got something written on it. I wish I could read better, it might be a letter. P-O-E-M-po-em! (*Calls into house.*) My lady, somebody's thrown a po-em into the loggetta!

   ROSAURA *comes out into loggetta.*

ROSAURA: A poem? Who could have done that?

COLUMBINA: I don't know. There was nobody here when I came out.

ROSAURA: Give it me.

COLUMBINA (*handing her the paper*): I must go and finish the ironing while the iron's hot. Please, my lady, do come and tell me what it says – when you've read it. (*Goes into house.*)

   ROSAURA *stands reading the poem in the loggetta.* LELIO *enters back right and comes down front right.*

LELIO (*aside*): Rosaura seems to be reading something with great interest. I wonder what it is?

ROSAURA (*aside*): But who on earth could have written this?

LELIO (*going centre*): May I be allowed the pleasure of saluting the Signora? (*He bows.*)

ROSAURA: I beg your pardon, my lord. I did not see you.

LELIO: Might I be permitted to know what you are reading so attentively?

ROSAURA: It is a poem that Columbina found in the loggetta

here. It's addressed to me, but there's no name of the
sender.

LELIO (*stepping closer to loggetta*): You don't recognize the
handwriting even?

ROSAURA: No. I certainly *should* like to know who wrote it.
I've been trying to guess but I've no idea who it could be.

LELIO: So – it's quite a good poem, then?

ROSAURA: Yes: *I* think it is.

LELIO (*moving thoughtfully back to front centre*): It – er – it
wouldn't be a (*he pauses and turns towards her*) love poem,
would it?

ROSAURA: As a matter of fact – it is!

LELIO: And you *still* have no idea who wrote it?

ROSAURA: No, absolutely none.

LELIO: Look a little closer. (*Goes nearer loggetta.*)

ROSAURA: D'you mean – it's you who wrote it?

LELIO: A poor thing – but all mine own.

ROSAURA: You amaze me!

LELIO: Why? Didn't you think I was capable of writing a
poem?

ROSAURA: Yes – but – well, not exactly one like this! Listen!
(*She reads.*)
  'Queen of my heart, goddess divine,
   For love of you, Rosaura mine,
   In silence I suffer and pine.'

LELIO (*moving down right*): Quite good, really, don't you
think?

   'Queen of my heart, goddess divine,
    For love of you, Rosaura mine,
    In silence I suffer and pine.'

You see, I know it by heart.

ROSAURA: Yes, but why 'in silence' when you spoke to me yesterday and this morning?

LELIO: Ah, but remember, I have been silent for a whole year nearly.

ROSAURA: Well – perhaps you can explain this—

> 'No lord am I, no proud titles mine,
> My profession is my only sign
> Of rank or wealth, Rosaura mine.'

LELIO (*aside, down right*): Here's a confounded mess!

ROSAURA: I'm waiting, my lord. How could you have written those lines?

LELIO (*moving centre*): Signora, I have a confession to make. It is true. I am no lord. It was a fantastic invention on my part – and then lacking the courage to tell you, I thought of telling you the truth like this – in a poem. Nor am I rich. In Naples I am a merchant, so it is quite true that 'my profession is my only sign of rank or wealth'.

ROSAURA: Well! I really should have nothing more to do with you. But, after all, an honest merchant is as good as many a nobleman. So I suppose I must forgive you. Still, the rest of the poem does puzzle me a little also.

LELIO (*aside, moving back down right*): The devil! What else is there?

ROSAURA (*reading*): 'Oh, how often you see me near you.' But I never saw you before last night, so how can you say 'How often you see me near you'?

LELIO: Did I really say it in those words, 'how often *you* see me'?

ROSAURA: Yes.

LELIO (*moving centre*): How silly of me. It was a slip of the pen. I meant to say, 'How often *you'll* see me'. The future tense and not the present tense, of course.

ROSAURA: Well, there are still the last four lines.

LELIO (*aside, moving back down right*): If I get out of this, it'll be a miracle!

ROSAURA (*reading*):

> 'Only for your sake I in Venice live,
> Far, far from Lombardy whence I came.'

How can you come from Lombardy if you come from Naples?

LELIO: Naples is part of Lombardy.

ROSAURA: What! The Kingdom of Naples is in the province of Lombardy?

LELIO (*coming centre*): You will recall that formerly the Lombards conquered all Italy, and hence Italy is often referred to – in poetry – as Lombardy.

ROSAURA: Well, it may be as you say. But what about the last line? (*Reads.*) 'Soon, to you, will I reveal my name.'

LELIO (*stepping front centre and declaiming with such conviction that he apparently believes it himself*): Which I now shall do. Know then that I am not Fernando of Castel d'Oro, but Ruggiero Pandolfi, merchant, of Naples.

ROSAURA: Well, I certainly would never have understood the poem without these explanations.

LELIO: Ah, but you must remember we poets nearly always speak in metaphors and figures of speech.

ROSAURA: So even – your name – was a figure of speech?

LELIO: Last night I was in a poetic mood.

ROSAURA: And what mood are you in today?

LELIO: Today I am in the mood of literal and prosaic truth.

ROSAURA: And you still wish to speak to my father?

LELIO: I shall never find peace until he has given his consent. Where can I find him?

ROSAURA: Here he comes now!

DOCTOR (*to* ROSAURA *from just within the house*): Is that he?
ROSAURA: Yes, but—
DOCTOR: Then come in at once.
ROSAURA: But listen—
DOCTOR: Do as I say! I don't want to hear anything more from you yet.

He draws her into the house and they both disappear.

LELIO (*aside*): Really, I carried that off extremely well. There's not many could have got themselves out of such a mix-up.

Stands preening himself down right, and then starts making mock polite conversation to an imaginary listener.

The DOCTOR *comes out of his house by the door, unobserved by* LELIO.

DOCTOR (*aside, down left*): Yes, you can see from his manner he's a great nobleman, but he seems to me to be a little eccentric. (LELIO *sees him and assumes a very serious air.*)

LELIO (*aside*): Here goes. (*Aloud, moving right centre.*) Doctor, your most devoted servant. (*Bows.*)

DOCTOR (*moving left centre and bowing*): Your most humble servant, my lord.

LELIO: Are you not, sir, the father of the Signora Rosaura?

DOCTOR: At your service, my lord.

LELIO: Sir, I am a man who does not beat about the bush. So, without further ado, permit me to say that I have been captivated by your daughter's charms, and that I wish to marry her.

DOCTOR: My lord, I like your straightforward way of speaking. My answer is that you do my family an honour which is far above our station. I shall willingly give my consent when you have had the opportunity – and condescension – to prove your identity.

OTTAVIO *comes out of the Inn and, on seeing* LELIO, *comes angrily between him and the* DOCTOR.

OTTAVIO: So there you are! (*Flicks him across the cheek with his hand.*) Take that – for speaking these wicked lies about the Doctor's daughters. And now, *if* you're a gentleman, you'll draw your sword.

DOCTOR (*retreating down left*): Ottavio, what are you doing?! My lord Marquis has just . . .

OTTAVIO: My lord Marquis – my foot! This is Lelio – Signor Pantalone's son.

DOCTOR: The devil it is!

LELIO (*to* OTTAVIO): Whoever I am, I've spirit enough to cut your cackle, my fine rooster. (*Draws his sword.*)

OTTAVIO (*drawing his sword*): Let's see if you can lie your way out of this!

DOCTOR: Put up your sword, Ottavio. I forbid you to fight with this – this detestable liar. Come with me at once!

OTTAVIO: Leave us, I beg you, sir.

DOCTOR: Do as I say, sir! If you wish to marry Beatrice, you will come with me! (*Goes into his house.*)

OTTAVIO (*to* LELIO, *lowering his sword*): We'll meet again, you and I.

LELIO: Always ready to oblige. Any time or place you like. (OTTAVIO *goes into house after the* DOCTOR.) The devil take him! He's spoilt everything! By heaven, I'll make him pay for this! (*Stands waving his sword and posturing before an imaginary adversary.*) With this sword, you dog, I shall make you regret having insulted me in such a manner! Ah! You would, would you! Take that, you snake-in-the-grass!

ARLECCHINO *has come out of* PANTALONE'S *house and is standing watching him.*

ARLECCHINO: Eh, master! What are you waving your sword about like that for?

LELIO: It was Ottavio. He dared to challenge me.

ARLECCHINO: You *haven't* had a fight with him?

LELIO: For a good three-quarters of an hour!

ARLECCHINO: Lord! What happened?

LELIO: Ah! With one stroke I finally pierced him from side to side.

ARLECCHINO: But that would have killed him!

LELIO: Naturally!

ARLECCHINO: Eeeh! What've you done with it?

LELIO: Done with what?

ARLECCHINO: The body!

LELIO (*carelessly*): Oh, they've taken it away.

ARLECCHINO: And to think I've gone and missed it all!

 OTTAVIO *comes out of the* DOCTOR'S *house.*

OTTAVIO (*to* LELIO): Don't think I've done with *you*, yet! I'll be on the Giudecca tomorrow morning at nine o'clock. If you are a man of honour you will fight me there.

 At the sight of OTTAVIO, ARLECCHINO *has pretended to be full of admiration for* LELIO.

LELIO: I'll be there, don't doubt that.

OTTAVIO: Good! I'll teach you to go about telling lies about people!

 Exit back right.

ARLECCHINO: Glory be! I've seen a dead man walking!

LELIO: Oh, don't be silly. It's just that – well, I was so blinded with rage, I must have killed somebody else!

ARLECCHINO: What with? A witty invention!

 Laughing loudly, he runs off left quickly.

LELIO (*running after him waving his sword*): I'll show you what with, you impudent good-for-nothing knave!

MUSIC QUICK CURTAIN

Scene II

Late afternoon of the same day.

FLORINDO enters back right and stands centre looking fondly at the loggetta.

FLORINDO: Ah, my dear little loggetta. How lonely you look! Like me, you wait and wait, and she never comes.

  BRIGHELLA *enters left.*

BRIGHELLA: Ah, there you are, sir! I was hoping I'd find you.

FLORINDO (*despondently*): Were you, Brighella?

BRIGHELLA: After you dashed off like that I met the servant of this Marquis of Castel d'Oro.

FLORINDO: Well?

BRIGHELLA: Well, according to his servant, this here Marquis has been reaping what you've sown but haven't got the courage to reap yourself.

FLORINDO: What *are* you talking about, Brighella? Oh, why does everything seem so hopeless!

BRIGHELLA: Quite proud of his master, he was, as well. A right couple, they are, if you ask me.

FLORINDO: For pity's sake, Brighella, tell me – what is it that his servant told you?

BRIGHELLA: Quite simple. You sends my lady some lace – right?

FLORINDO: Of course! You ordered it yourself.

BRIGHELLA: Aye, with strict instructions that *your* name wasn't to be mentioned. So this here Marquis tells the Signora Rosaura that *he* sent her the lace.

FLORINDO: Oh, no!

BRIGHELLA: You haven't heard the half of it yet. You sends

her a poem. But she's not to know it comes from you.
Right? So what does this here Marquis do? Why, he tells
her that *he* sent her the poem, as well.

FLORINDO: Oh, this is terrible! Whatever am I to do?

BRIGHELLA: I have a plan. Look, let us go into the house
and I'll tell you what it is.

FLORINDO: Yes, of course. My dear Brighella, I'm so
grateful to you. If ever I do marry Rosaura, I shall owe it to
you.

    Both go into DOCTOR'S *house.*

    ARLECCHINO *comes out of the Inn reading a letter. He turns
and calls back into the Inn.*

ARLECCHINO: Waiter!

WAITER (*coming out of the Inn*): Yes, sir?

ARLECCHINO: You've really no idea who brought this
letter?

WAITER: No, sir. Like I told you, sir, somebody left it on this
table here. I saw it was addressed to the Count Obstinato
of Catalania. So I kept it for you, sir. Would that be all, sir?
Would your Excellency like some coffee, perhaps?

ARLECCHINO: Yes, I certainly could do with a cup of coffee.
Bring it out here, will you?

WAITER: Yes, sir. (*He goes into the Inn.*)

ARLECCHINO (*looking at the letter again*): Well, I've never
had a letter like this before. From an unknown lady, who
says she will come, masked, to the Inn here to see me. And
that I'll know her by the red ribbons on her dress. (*He looks
across at the* DOCTOR'S *house.*) I wonder if somebody's
having me on? If they are, I think I've got a good idea who
it is.

    COLUMBINA *enters back left. She is masked and is wearing
a short green cloak with red ribbons.*

Here's a masked girl now. And she's got red ribbons as

well! (*To* COLUMBINA.) Your servant, Signora. I was wondering whether you'd turn up.

COLUMBINA (*frigidly*): Are you by any chance speaking to me?

ARLECCHINO (*looking round*): I don't see anyone else here.

COLUMBINA (*superciliously*): Do you know me?

ARLECCHINO: As a matter of fact, I don't – yet.

COLUMBINA: Gentlemen do not speak to masked ladies whom they do not know.

ARLECCHINO: Well, in a manner of speaking, of course, I do know you. By the – er – token.

COLUMBINA: Token? What token?

ARLECCHINO: By those red ribbons you're wearing.

COLUMBINA (*going left stage*): Good gracious, sir, many ladies in Venice wear red ribbons. (*She steps down left and rearranges the ribbons.*) I am not the only one who wears ribbons like these.

ARLECCHINO (*aside, down right*): From her voice, I'll swear it's that maid Columbina. (*Aloud.*) Most charming, and mysterious, masked lady! May I venture to offer you some coffee?

COLUMBINA: What *are* you saying, sir! If my husband came by, I shudder to think what would happen!

ARLECCHINO (*incredulously*): You're *married*!

COLUMBINA: With six children, sir. Two boys and four girls.

ARLECCHINO (*aside, down right*): It's not her, then. (*Aloud, coming centre.*) Then you aren't the lady who wrote me this letter?

COLUMBINA: I, sir? But I cannot read or write. (*Aside.*) My mistress wrote it.

ARLECCHINO (*disappointedly, moving right again*): Oh. You're only a common woman then?

COLUMBINA: How dare you, sir! You would regret speaking thus if you knew who it is under this mask!

ARLECCHINO (*aside – right stage*): But you said you couldn't read or write!

COLUMBINA (*with a toss of her head – still down left*): I say what I please to impertinent busybodies!

ARLECCHINO (*aside – down right – desperately*): This is getting me all hot and bothered. (*Aloud, coming centre.*) Please! Just tell me – on your word of honour – did you or didn't you write me this letter?

COLUMBINA: On my word of honour, Count Obstinato, I did not write that letter.

ARLECCHINO (*going back right*): In that case I am sorry to have— (*He stops with his back to the audience, shoulders hunched in a double-take, and then swings round to her again.*) *What* was that you said?

COLUMBINA: I said I did not write that letter.

ARLECCHINO: No, no, not that! What was it you called me?

COLUMBINA: Why, Count Obstinato, of course.

ARLECCHINO: You know me then?

COLUMBINA: Of course.

ARLECCHINO: You've seen me before?

COLUMBINA: Oh, yes. And spoken to you.

ARLECCHINO: Where? When?

COLUMBINA: Do you know – I really just can't remember.
She walks back right as though going. ARLECCHINO *quickly blocks her way, speaking with desperate determination.*

ARLECCHINO: *You're* making fun of *me*! Take that mask off and stop playing this cat and mouse game!
The WAITER *comes out of the Inn with coffee-pot and cups on a tray.*

WAITER: Here is the coffee, sir. I've brought an extra cup as

I saw you had company. (*He puts the tray on the table right, gives* ARLECCHINO *a wink, and goes back into the Inn.*)

COLUMBINA (*going right*): Do you know – I think I'll have a cup of coffee after all. (*She sits at table right.*) If my husband does see me, he'll only run his sword through you.

ARLECCHINO (*his hand shaking as he pours out the coffee*): Look – I'm a peaceful chap and I don't like causing any trouble. Not that I believe you're married, anyway.

COLUMBINA (*pointedly disregarding what he is saying*): Oh, a little more sugar – if you wouldn't mind.

ARLECCHINO (*heaping sugar into her cup*): I said, of course I don't believe you *are* married, anyway.

COLUMBINA (*forgetting herself*): Eh, hold on! That's enough of the sugar!

ARLECCHINO: Well, you'll have to take it off now, that's certain. You can't drink your coffee with that mask on.

COLUMBINA: Oh, but I can, you know. It only needs a bit of practice. (*She takes a sip and puts the cup on the table.*) Coffee, at Inns, always seems to taste better than coffee made at home, don't you think?

ARLECCHINO (*goaded to desperation*): Look – I can't stand this any longer! If you won't take that thing off your face – then *I* will! (*He reaches to take her mask away and she gives him a resounding box on the ear.*) OW! That hurt! What d'you want to go and do that for!

COLUMBINA *rises and seems to say something, but in fact only makes motions with her lips without really saying anything.*

ARLECCHINO: What's that you say?

COLUMBINA *repeats the mime as above.*

ARLECCHINO: I can't hear you! Speak a little louder!

COLUMBINA – *as above.*

ARLECCHINO (*shouting*): I said I can't hear you! Speak louder – into my ear!

COLUMBINA *goes to him and appears to shout down his ear.*

ARLECCHINO: The devil! I've gone stone-deaf! Try the other side!

COLUMBINA *goes round him and appears to shout something down his other ear.*

ARLECCHINO: Good heavens, I'm absolutely deaf! I can't hear a word you say!

COLUMBINA *again moves her lips as though saying something, and then goes off left stage.*

ARLECCHINO (*calling after her*): Come back! You can't leave me like this! Come back and tell me who you are! (*To himself.*) What am I saying? Perhaps she did tell me! I couldn't hear a thing she said.

The WAITER *comes out of the Inn.*

WAITER: Did you call, sir?

ARLECCHINO (*without turning*): No, no, I wasn't calling you!

WAITER: I beg your pardon, sir. (*He turns to go back into the Inn.*)

ARLECCHINO (*turning to him*): Wait! What did you say?

WAITER: I asked if you had called me, sir.

ARLECCHINO: Now I can hear, and yet just now I couldn't. There's something fishy about this. Waiter, you wouldn't happen to know who that young lady is – who was here just now – would you?

WAITER: Why, of course, sir. That was Columbina, from that house over there. She's maidservant to the Doctor's daughters – aye, and a sharp-tongued little madam she is, too. Have you finished with the coffee, sir?

ARLECCHINO: What? Oh, yes, you can take it away. (WAITER *takes tray into the Inn.*) Take everything away! What does anything matter now? She was laughing at me. She thinks I'm only a fool. Oh, unhappy Arlecchino! How will you go on living without her? Let us hasten away and die. Let it be written in the history books that Arlecchino died for love of Columbina! (*To the audience.*) Give me a rope, somebody, that I may endure this agony no longer.... (*When these dots occur* ARLECCHINO *skips from one part to the other, changing his voice and gestures.*) ... A rope? Fie, sir, what are you thinking of? Die for the sake of a maid-servant? What sort of madness is that? ... True, sir, but even a maidservant should not laugh at the love of an honest man.... Agreed, but when you're dead will you be any better off? ... No, I'll be worse off, but that suits me; you can come and join me if you like.... What, me? No, thanks! And I'm not going to let *you* do it either. ... Oh, yes, you are! ... Oh, no, I'm not! ... Oh, yes, you are; so get out of my way. (*He beats himself with his baton.*) There, that's driven *him* away; now, there's nobody to stop me. Well, if no one'll give me a rope, I'll find one myself. (*He starts walking off left and then stops.*) No. After all, hanging's such an ordinary thing – it happens every day. I must try and think of an heroic death – a really extraordinary one. (*He thinks.*) I've got it! I'll hold my nose, and put my hand over my mouth, and then I won't be able to breathe. Why, it's as good as done! (*He holds his nose with one hand and puts the other tightly over his mouth. After a moment he gives up with a loud explosion and inhalations of air.*) That was more difficult than I thought. Wait! Ah, now I've really got it! I'm always hearing of people nearly dying of laughing. And I'm certainly a very ticklish sort of person. Yes, if somebody tickled me long enough, I'm sure I'd die of laughing. I'll try it on myself. (*He tickles himself, begins to laugh and falls to the ground. He starts rolling round the stage, tickling himself vigorously and roaring with helpless laughter.* PANTALONE *comes out of his house – carrving the letter for posting – and,*

seeing ARLECCHINO *in this state, believes him to be drunk.*)
PANTALONE (*shouting*): You! What's your name – Arlecchino? Been helping yourself to my wine, have you, you
drunken rascal! (*He pulls* ARLECCHINO *to his feet by lifting
him under the armpits. This starts* ARLECCHINO *whooping
with helpless laughter again.*)
You thieving rogue, I'll teach you to steal my wine! (*He
starts beating him with his stick.* ARLECCHINO'S *laughter
changes to shouts of pain and he scurries off back right, chased by*
PANTALONE. PANTALONE *returns centre stage.*)
(*Out of breath.*) I shouldn't wonder if it's that fellow who's
been putting my son up to his own knavish tricks. Where
on earth could he have picked up such a fool of a servant?
(*Looks at letter in his hand.*) Yes, and I don't want any
servant forgetting about this, so I'd best post it myself. I
should have written long ago. What on earth will the girl's
father think of me? Eh – he's a silly lad, that son of mine,
if he's let that fool of a servant put him up to all these tricks
the Doctor's been telling me about. Marquis of Castel
d'Oro, indeed! I'll give him Marquis! Making a fool of
the Doctor's daughters and him with a newly-wedded wife
in Naples! I'll give his 'Lordship' a talking-to when I've
posted this letter!
　　A LETTER-CARRIER *enters left.*
LETTER-CARRIER: A letter for you, Signor Pantalone.
Thirty soldini to pay.
PANTALONE: Where's it from?
LETTER-CARRIER: From the post at Naples.
PANTALONE: Here's your money. (*Takes letter and gives him
money.*)
LETTER-CARRIER: I beg your pardon, sir, but d'you happen
to know a Signor Lelio Bisognosi?
PANTALONE: Why, he's my son – just arrived from Naples.

LETTER-CARRIER: Well, here's one for him too – but it's from Rome.

PANTALONE: I'll take it, then. He stayed at Rome on his journey back here. How much?

LETTER-CARRIER: Fifteen soldini, sir.

PANTALONE: Here you are. (*Gives him money and takes the letter.*)

LETTER-CARRIER: Thank'ee, sir. (*Exit left.*)

PANTALONE: Who can be writing to me from Naples? I don't know the handwriting. (*Opens letter.*) Let's see who it's from. (*Turns letter over and reads.*) 'Masaniello Cappezali'? Never heard of him. What's *he* want? (*Turns letter over again and reads.*) 'Dear Sir, I have written twice to your son, and, having had no answer, I fear he may be ill. I am therefore writing to you, enclosing the Bachelor's Certificate which Lelio asked me to obtain for him, so that he might be able to marry, if he wished, after his return to Venice.'

What *is* all this? His certificate as a bachelor? Yes, here it is. (*Looks at another paper he has taken out of the envelope.*) *And* it seems to be quite in order. Then he's not married – or is this some practical joke? I must get to the bottom of this. Let's see if this other letter explains what all this is about.

    He is starting to open LELIO'S *letter when* LELIO *enters back right.*

LELIO: Ah, there you are, Father. I was just coming to look for you.

PANTALONE: Do you know somebody called Masaniello Cappezali?

LELIO: Masaniello? Oh, yes! (*Moving right.*) A great friend of mine in Naples.

PANTALONE: He's an honest man? Doesn't go in for – practical jokes?

LELIO: Not any more, alas!

PANTALONE: No? Why not?

LELIO: The poor fellow is dead. (*Aside, down right.*) He's best out of the way. My father might write to him. (PANTALONE *is having another look at the letter.*)

PANTALONE (*slowly*): When – did he die?

LELIO: Oh, quite a time ago. Long before I left Naples.

PANTALONE (*slowly*): More than – three months ago, then?

LELIO: Oh, yes, more like six months ago.

PANTALONE (*mock cheerfully*): Well, I've a bit of good news for you, lad. He's come alive again.

LELIO: What?

PANTALONE (*going with great deliberation down right and standing on* LELIO'S *right*): Is *that* his handwriting?

LELIO (*crossing left after glancing at the letter*): Oh, no, nothing like it! (*Aside, down left.*) It is an' all – what's going on?

PANTALONE (*down right*): You're quite sure this isn't his handwriting?

LELIO (*down left*): Positive – besides, I told you, he's dead.

PANTALONE (*aside, down right*): Either this letter's a joke or my son's the father of all liars. I must find out the truth.

LELIO (*aside, down left*): I must find out what's in that letter. (*Aloud, coming centre.*) Father, may I have a closer look at that handwriting?

PANTALONE (*coming centre*): *Is* the poor gentleman dead – or isn't he?

LELIO: Of course he is.

PANTALONE: He's dead – and you're *certain* of it. We'll leave that, then, for the moment. There's another matter. What've you been up to with the Doctor's daughter, Signora Rosaura?

LELIO: I like that! What's *she* been up to with me, would be more like it.

PANTALONE: Heaven give me patience! What can the Signora Rosaura have done to you?

LELIO: Ruined me, that's all.

PANTALONE (*stepping back in astonishment*): *Ruined* you?!

LELIO (*crossing, in front of* PANTALONE, *down right*): What else? She looked at me with those two eyes of hers and I was done for on the spot.

PANTALONE(*following him*): She looked at you! She *looked* at you! And so you had to invite yourself into the Doctor's house and order a huge meal to be brought in? And you a married man!

LELIO: You're right, Father. I shouldn't have done it. It will never happen again. (*Stands preening himself self-righteously.*)

PANTALONE (*moving centre, thumping angrily with his stick*): What makes it all the worse for me is that the Signora Rosaura is the young lady I meant you to marry.

LELIO (*his self-righteous pose completely punctured*): WHO? Who did you say she is?

PANTALONE: Why, the young lady I had arranged for you to marry.

LELIO: But – why on earth didn't you tell me?

PANTALONE: Because what with all these fairy-tale complications of yours, you never gave me the chance. Anyway, what difference does it make now? You're a married man, aren't you?

LELIO (*aside, returning down right*): Lord! What've I done now?

PANTALONE: What's that you say?

LELIO (*turning to him*): Father, I cannot live without her!

PANTALONE: Without who?

LELIO: The Signora Rosaura!

PANTALONE: The devil take it – how many wives *do* you want?

LELIO: One is all I ask! Just one!

PANTALONE: Well, you've got your Briseide, haven't you?

LELIO: Alas, Father!

PANTALONE: Now don't tell me she's gone and died, as well.

LELIO (*kneeling*): Behold me, Father, at your feet.

PANTALONE: Oh, get up! What's coming now?

LELIO: I am *not* married. There is no such person as Briseide.

PANTALONE: Just as I suspected! Well, that finishes it. First of all, you're the Marquis of Castel d'Oro – why didn't you make yourself King of Naples while you were at it? – and then you let me write a letter to your father-in-law who don't exist. Where d'you get it all from! Where d'you learn all these fairy-tales? *And how the devil d'you make them up so dam' quick?*

LELIO: It was all for the sake of Rosaura, Father. When I thought you wanted me to marry another, I had to *think* quickly and before I knew what I was doing, I was making up all these – all these fairy-tales.

PANTALONE: And you really aren't married?

LELIO: Certainly not.

PANTALONE: Not even engaged?

LELIO: No. Not even engaged.

PANTALONE: And Masaniello Cappezali? – I suppose that was another of your fairy-tales and this bachelor's certificate is quite genuine?

LELIO: My bachelor's certificate? He's sent it to you?

PANTALONE: He thought it safer in case you had not arrived yet. So your friend isn't dead?

LELIO: I'm afraid I thought you might write to him and so find out I was not married.

PANTALONE: Well, here you are, then. (*Gives him the bachelor's certificate and moves right centre.*) And if there's to be no more of these fairy-tales, I'll have a talk with the

Doctor and see what can be done. Oh! Here's this letter which came for you.

LELIO: For me? (*Going to him, right.*)

PANTALONE: Ay, from Rome. I paid fifteen soldini for it.

LELIO (*holding out his hand for it*): Thank you very much, Father.

PANTALONE *crosses in front of* LELIO, *ignoring his out-stretched hand and begins opening the letter, down left.*

PANTALONE: By your leave, I'm your father and I mean to read it.

LELIO: As you wish. (*Aside, down right.*) I hope this isn't another complication!

PANTALONE (*reading*): 'My darling husband—' (*he double-takes and chokes*) HUSBAND!

LELIO: It can't be for me, then.

PANTALONE: It's addressed to you! And it's signed (*reading*) 'Your most loving and faithful *wife*, Cleonice'.

LELIO: Well, that proves it's not for me.

PANTALONE: What does?

LELIO: I don't even know the lady.

PANTALONE (*with forced patience*): And who d'you suppose it's meant for, then?

LELIO: Why, somebody else with the same name!

PANTALONE (*moving centre*): I've lived in Venice all my life and never heard of any others with our name.

LELIO: Oh, I've met people in Naples – and in Rome – with our name.

PANTALONE (*almost losing control of himself*): But the letter was sent *here* – to Venice!

LELIO: Well, somebody of my name *from* Rome or Naples *could* be here in Venice, *couldn't* they?

PANTALONE *gazes at him almost in awe.*

PANTALONE (*after a pause*): Yes – maybe they could at that. Let's see what it says.

LELIO: Excuse me, sir, but it's not quite right to read another person's letters.

PANTALONE: I told you, I can read my son's letters and I intend to.

LELIO: But I thought we'd just proved that it wasn't mine.

PANTALONE (*impatiently – moving down left again*): We'll see about that!

LELIO (*aside*): Oh, lord, my witty inventions are just about drying up!

PANTALONE (*reading*): 'Your departure from Rome has plunged me into melancholy, for after all you did promise to take me with you to Venice.'

LELIO: There you are, I told you it wasn't for me.

PANTALONE: But it says 'take me with you to *Venice*'!

LELIO: *All* right – he's *in* Venice! *So* what?

PANTALONE (*reading*): 'You promised to marry me, and if you break your promise, I shall write to your father, Signor Pantalone Bisognosi.' Pantalone, eh? What d'you make of that?

LELIO (*crossing to him down left, attempting now to laugh the matter off*): Just fancy that! The father's name is the same, too. I'd never have believed it!

PANTALONE: Let's hear the end of it. (*Reads.*) 'And I am sure he will not wish to see you in prison for taking money from me on account of my dowry.' Well, now I have heard everything! There just could not be anything any worse than this!

LELIO (*with a forced laugh*): Yes, it certainly does appear that some friend of mine has got a strange sense of humour.

PANTALONE (*exploding*): Humour? Humour? I'll humour *you*, my lad. You don't set foot inside my house again! You can have the money and get off back to Rome and marry the girl!

LELIO: Oh, but, Father . . .

PANTALONE: Don't you 'father' me. I'm no father of a bare-faced, blackguard of a liar! (*Goes angrily into his house.*)

LELIO: But, Father, I don't want to tell lies, really. I do so much want always to tell the truth. It's just that – well, you see – the truth never seems to get me what I want. Don't you understand? Telling lies always seems so much easier.

LELIO *sits dejectedly at the Inn table right.* FLORINDO *and* BRIGHELLA *come out of the* DOCTOR'S *house.* BRIGHELLA *goes over to* LELIO, *leaving* FLORINDO *down left.*

BRIGHELLA: Sir, my master wishes to inform you that you are either a liar or a looney.

LELIO (*listlessly*): Then you can tell your master that he's an impertinent rascal.

BRIGHELLA (*disconcerted*): Is that all?

LELIO: You can tell him he's an impudent knave as well, if you like.

BRIGHELLA: But aren't you going to demand satisfaction?

LELIO: From whom?

BRIGHELLA: From my master.

LELIO: How?

BRIGHELLA: Why, with your sword, of course.

LELIO: Look, old man, just tell your master that I have more important things to think about at the moment. If he really wishes to be taught a lesson in good manners, I shall be glad to oblige him at some other time.

BRIGHELLA *goes across left to* FLORINDO.

BRIGHELLA: He took it all lying down, master. You'll have to go over and insult him yourself.

FLORINDO: Yes – but what if—

BRIGHELLA (*pushing him towards* LELIO): It's the only way, believe me, master.

FLORINDO (*to* LELIO): Your servant, sir. Er – pray excuse me if I seem over-sensitive about my honour. But if you refuse to give me satisfaction, sir, I shall have no alternative but to have you run out of town.

LELIO (*rising*): Sir, honest men cannot be run out of town as easily as that.

FLORINDO: Sir, you are an impudent scoundrel who has been doing harm to my good name. What's more, I very much doubt whether you are what you call yourself.

LELIO: Call myself? I am Ruggiero Pandolfi, merchant, of Naples. What else should I call myself?

FLORINDO: Then you are not the Marquis of Castel d'Oro?

LELIO: My dear sir! What on earth can have given you that idea? Ah! That servant of yours has perhaps been spinning you some tale! (*Raising his voice.*) The poor old man certainly looks a little – er – you know. (*He taps his head and receives a glare from* BRIGHELLA *down left.*)

FLORINDO: I beg your pardon, sir. 'Tis true, it was indeed my servant who gave me to understand that you were this person whom I wish to challenge.

LELIO: There is no harm done, sir. Mistakes often occur (*raising his voice*) especially when a servant becomes old and doddery. (*Glare from* BRIGHELLA.)

FLORINDO: If you will excuse me, sir, I will go and ask my servant how he came to make such a mistake. My most humble apologies, sir.

LELIO: Pray do not beat the old fellow; 'tis of no account, I assure you. (*Suitable expressive reaction from* BRIGHELLA *down left.*)

FLORINDO: I am much obliged to you. Your servant, sir.

LELIO: Yours to command, sir.

    They bow to each other. FLORINDO *goes across to* BRIGHELLA *and leads him off, left,* BRIGHELLA *expostulating violently. As soon as they have gone,* ARLECCHINO *enters, back right.*

ARLECCHINO: Oh, sir! I've just heard that a young lady has arrived in Venice, looking for you. It must be that one from Rome – you know who.

LELIO: Cleonice? It can't be!

ARLECCHINO: Well, who else can it be, sir. I hear she's putting up at the Crown Inn, and has been asking where your father lives.

LELIO: We'd better hide in this Inn, then – while I try to think of something before she gets here.

ARLECCHINO: If I was you, master, I'd make a clean breast of it all – go and ask the Doctor to forgive you.

LELIO: Yes, I might be able to bluff it out like that. I'll tell you what. I'll go into the Inn out of the way and think it over. You go and keep an eye out for Cleonice. If you hear she's on her way here, try to come and warn me.

ARLECCHINO: I'll do my best, sir. You can rely on me.

LELIO: Good! (*He goes into the Inn.*)

ARLECCHINO: Though if you ask me, these capers of yours can't go on much longer. I always said he'd go too far with those witty inventions of his.

> *Exit back right.*

> ROSAURA *comes out of the* DOCTOR'S *house and looks left and then back right. The* DOCTOR *enters left.*

DOCTOR: Well, daughter? Are you still looking for the Marquis of Castel d'Oro, as he calls himself?

ROSAURA (*coming right centre*): It may surprise you to know, Father, but I'm well aware that he is not a Marquis.

DOCTOR: Oh, so you *do* know *that*, do you?

ROSAURA: Yes, Father. He has told me everything. He is Ruggiero Pandolfi, a Neapolitan merchant.

DOCTOR: Mm? Ruggiero Pandolfi, eh? He told you that, did he?

ROSAURA: Yes.

DOCTOR: A Neapolitan merchant, eh?

ROSAURA: That is correct.

DOCTOR: Rich, I suppose?

ROSAURA: Comfortably so, I believe.

DOCTOR (*exploding*): You half-witted girl! When will you learn some sense! Do you *really* want to know who he is?

ROSAURA: What d'you mean? I've just told you.

DOCTOR: Neapolitan merchant? Pah! He's nothing of the sort. He's Lelio – Lelio Bisognosi!

ROSAURA: Signor Pantalone's son?

DOCTOR: Exactly!

ROSAURA: The man you proposed marrying me to?

DOCTOR: The same.

ROSAURA: Then – surely – things have turned out just as you wanted.

DOCTOR: Just as I wanted! He introduces himself to you under a false name because he's already got a wife in Rome! D'you think that's just what I wanted?

ROSAURA: I don't believe it!

DOCTOR: His father admitted it all to me – only half an hour ago.

ROSAURA: The scoundrel! The deceitful, lying scoundrel! Oh, what shall become of me now! (*Runs weeping into the house.*)

DOCTOR: Oh, dear, it's all too bad! I didn't like having to do that at all. But she had to be told. Now, I must try to think what's best to be done with her.

    OTTAVIO *enters back right.*

OTTAVIO: Sir, your maid has given me to understand that the Signora Beatrice wishes to speak to me. As I am a man of honour, I should like your permission before doing so.

DOCTOR: Ah, Ottavio, if only all young men were like you! Of course you may speak with Beatrice. We shall both go in and see what she has to say.

 LELIO *comes out of the Inn.*

LELIO (*right*): Sir, I come to beg your forgiveness.

DOCTOR (*centre*): Sir – you are a damned impostor!

OTTAVIO (*left*): Tomorrow I'm going to teach you a lesson you won't forget.

LELIO: But don't you understand – either of you? I want to be friends.

OTTAVIO: You? Who with?

LELIO: With both of you – but especially with the dear Doctor here.

DOCTOR: What are you after now?

LELIO: Your daughter's hand, sir.

DOCTOR: How *dare* you, sir! A married man like you!

LELIO: I? Married? Who *could* have told you that?

DOCTOR: Your father, sir, told me! He has had the painful duty of informing me that without his knowledge you have married a young lady named Briseide, the daughter of a very wealthy nobleman of Rome.

LELIO: Then I am very much afraid he was not telling the truth.

OTTAVIO (*crossing in front of the* DOCTOR): Don't you ever stop making them up?

DOCTOR (*coming forward, now left of* OTTAVIO): How can you, sir! Your father is the soul of honour!

LELIO: Well, you can see for yourself. Here's my Bachelor's Certificate, issued in Naples. (*He holds it out and* OTTAVIO *snatches it.*)

OTTAVIO (*looking at the paper*): He must really *be* telling the truth this time! (*To* DOCTOR.) This is certainly quite genuine, sir!

DOCTOR (*crossing to* LELIO): Good heavens! Then you really aren't married?

LELIO: Of *course* not!

DOCTOR: But why should Pantalone say you are?

LELIO: I'm afraid my father has regretted the marriage arrangement he made with you – for Rosaura and me.

DOCTOR: But why?

LELIO: Because – in the piazza this morning – a marriage-broker, who had learnt of my arrival in Venice, offered him a dowry of 50,000 ducats for me.

DOCTOR: Signor Pantalone would never insult me like that!

LELIO: Greed blinds the best of us sometimes, you know.

DOCTOR: And you want to marry my daughter so much that you would refuse a dowry of 50,000 ducats?

LELIO: Yes, sir.

OTTAVIO *whispers something to the* DOCTOR.

DOCTOR: You're right, Ottavio. (*To* LELIO.) This all seems very hard to believe considering you've only known my daughter for two days.

LELIO: For two months, sir.

DOCTOR: Two months! But you only arrived yesterday!

LELIO: Sir, do you know how long it is since I left Naples?

DOCTOR: Your father told me that you left Naples three months ago – and that you stopped in Rome on the way for over two months.

LELIO: That is not true. I did not stop in Rome. I came straight here to Venice.

DOCTOR: Your father did not know of this?

OTTAVIO: Signor Lelio, you're an even bigger liar than I thought you were. *I* have been staying at the Eagle Inn for nearly a year, and I know that you didn't arrive there until yesterday.

LELIO: Ah, but what *you* don't know is that I had been staying here at the *Crown* Inn for two months. I decided to move yesterday, here to the *Eagle* Inn to be nearer Rosaura.

DOCTOR: But what *I can't* understand is why you had to invent that story about the supper last night?

LELIO: Well – to tell the truth, sir – I'm afraid I said that because it was the sort of thing I should *like* to have done. Oh, I know I've said a lot of foolish things, but you must believe that I really am the son of Signor Pantalone.

DOCTOR (*plaintively*): I just don't know! Even that may not be true!

LELIO: But there is my certificate!

DOCTOR: If it's genuine.

LELIO: Signor Ottavio agreed that it was.

OTTAVIO: Well, it seems to be.

LELIO: And after all, my marriage to the Signora Rosaura had already been arranged between my father and yourself.

DOCTOR: Yes, that's another thing. I don't like to think that Signor Pantalone would break his word for 50,000 ducats. Anyway, why doesn't he tell me himself?

LELIO: As a matter of fact – between ourselves – he hasn't the courage to.

DOCTOR: Well, if your father really meant to play that sort of trick on me, I'll certainly see that you marry her – yes, even if it's the last thing I do. Where is that certificate?

OTTAVIO: Here it is, sir.

DOCTOR (*taking it*): I'll go and fetch my daughter. If she still wants to marry you, then this will settle it. (*Goes into house.*)

OTTAVIO: Don't think you'll get away with *this*!

LELIO: What *do* you mean?

OTTAVIO: You'll find out tomorrow morning!

LELIO: But surely there's no need for us to fight now? I thought we were all friends again?

> *The* DOCTOR *and* ROSAURA *come out of the house. They are followed by* BEATRICE *and* COLUMBINA. *The* DOCTOR

brings ROSAURA *centre.* BEATRICE *stands by* OTTAVIO *down right.* COLUMBINA *remains back right.*

ROSAURA: But I thought you said he was married already?

DOCTOR: That was all a misunderstanding.

ROSAURA: Well, I told you *I* didn't believe he was, didn't I?

DOCTOR: Yes, yes! We'll forget all about that. It was all an unfortunate misunderstanding. The point is, now, do *you* want to marry *him*?

OTTAVIO: Take care, Signora, I must warn you, I shall not care to have this man as a brother-in-law.

ROSAURA: Well, if my sister's going to marry *you*, I don't see why I shouldn't marry *him*.

PANTALONE *comes out of his house.*

PANTALONE (*to* DOCTOR): What's all this? What's my son up to now?

DOCTOR: I'll tell you what your son's up to now, sir! He is giving me satisfaction for the way you have insulted me!

PANTALONE: Me? Insulted you? How have I insulted you?

LELIO (*coming quickly between them*): Come, that's all over and done with, now! Rosaura and I are to be married after all – so there's no need, Father, for you to apologize.

PANTALONE (*apoplectically*): Apologize! Me! You young scoundrel! I'll put paid to your little game! (*To* DOCTOR.) Read this, sir, and then tell me whether he's still going to marry your daughter. (*Gives* DOCTOR CLEONICE'S *letter.*)

LELIO: That letter, as I have already pointed out to my father, is addressed to somebody who appears to have the same name as myself.

DOCTOR (*looking up angrily from the letter*): So! You came straight to Venice, did you? Rosaura, stand away from that – that monster! He not only *did* stay in Rome but also got himself engaged to be married while he was there. To a young lady whose name (*he refers to the letter in his hand*) appears to be Cleonice Anselmi.

LELIO (*crossing to left centre*): It seems that you will force me to tell you the truth. As a matter of fact, I did happen to meet this young lady, Cleonice Anselmi, quite accidentally, during the three days that I spent in Rome. Unfortunately for me, she happens to be well known in Rome as a young lady who thinks that every young man she meets is dying to marry her.

OTTAVIO (*incredulously*): You know, I do believe he makes them up as he goes along!

FLORINDO *and* BRIGHELLA *come out of the Inn.*

FLORINDO: Doctor Balanzoni – please pardon my interrupting you – but there is something I must reveal to you about this man (*points to* LELIO) – and your daughters.

DOCTOR (*apoplectically*): But what more can he have been up to? In heaven's name, what else is there for me to know?

FLORINDO: Sir, this impostor has been claiming to have done, what in actual fact has been done by me. I would have the Signora Rosaura know that it was *I* who sent her the present of silk lace, and that it was *I* who wrote the poem which she received today.

LELIO: Liar!

FLORINDO (*holding out a sheet of paper*): This will soon show who is the liar. It is the rough draft of my poem in my own handwriting. The Signora Rosaura can tell us whether it is the poem which she received. (*He gives the paper to* ROSAURA.)

BRIGHELLA: Ay, sir, I can vouch for what Signor Florindo says. I saw him throw the poem into the loggetta myself.

ROSAURA: 'Tis indeed the very poem, Father, which I found in the loggetta this afternoon.

DOCTOR (*to* LELIO): And now, sir, I suppose you'll try and talk your way out of this?

LELIO: Me? Oh, no! I'm laughing my head off. This sentimental booby here writes a love poem, then throws it in
the loggetta and runs away and hides. And now that
Rosaura is mine, he decides to reveal himself. It's enough
to make me split my sides laughing.

PANTALONE (*raising his stick*): I'll split your sides for you all
right, you young—

DOCTOR (*restraining* PANTALONE): No, no, Signor Pantalone, let us all try to keep our tempers. (*To* LELIO.) Not
quite so fast, young man, if you please. (*To* FLORINDO.)
So, Florindo, am I to understand that you also wish to
marry my daughter, Rosaura?

FLORINDO: Indeed I do, sir. Until now I have lacked the
courage to say so.

ROSAURA: Oh, Florindo! And I've always thought you
didn't like me!

DOCTOR (*to* ROSAURA): Are we to take that to mean that
Florindo also pleases you?

ROSAURA: Oh, yes, Father! Oh, this is the happiest day of
my life! (*To* PANTALONE.) So you won't be too hard on
Lelio, will you, Signor Pantalone? Because, after all, if it
hadn't been for him, Florindo might never have found the
courage to tell me!

> ARLECCHINO *enters hastily back right and goes up to*
> LELIO.

ARLECCHINO (*to* LELIO): Hurry, master! There's no time
to lose!

LELIO: Please, Arlecchino, you're interrupting a most touch-
ing scene.

ARLECCHINO (*in a loud whisper*): Master – she's *here*!

PANTALONE: What is this fool talking about? Who's here?

ARLECCHINO: Oh, master, there's not time for a – for a witty
invention. That young lady from Rome is here!

LELIO: What? Cleonice?

CLEONICE *appears back right and advances purposefully upon* LELIO.

ARLECCHINO: It's too late, master! Here she is!

CLEONICE: So! I've found you! You sheep in wolf's clothing! You – ass in a lion's skin!

LELIO: Cleonice! Oh, how I've missed you!

CLEONICE: Liar! Cheat! Humbug! Swindler!

LELIO: Ah – how well you know me, my dear.

CLEONICE (*mock-romantic*): You fascinating charmer!

LELIO (*aside*): I'm done for! (*Aloud.*) You bewitching enchantress!

CLEONICE (*domineering again*): I'm hungry! I don't want to hear any of your lies until I've had a good meal.

LELIO: Allow me to escort you into this Inn, my love – and after you have had a good meal – I will tell you – the truth.

CLEONICE (*laughing*): And I'll never believe you!

They go arm in arm into the Inn. ARLECCHINO *crosses back right and stands by the Inn door looking lost and deserted.*

PANTALONE (*with astonished admiration*): Well! I must say, it looks as if that young lady knows how to handle him! (*He goes back right near* ARLECCHINO.)

DOCTOR: Thank goodness somebody has taken him off my hands. Let us all go into my house and we'll celebrate the engagement of Florindo and Rosaura and of Ottavio and Beatrice.

OTTAVIO (*a little sententiously*): Thank you, my dear Doctor Balanzoni. We are, indeed, four happy young people. And we, at any rate, owe our happiness and good fortune to our upright integrity.

Slow music begins. BRIGHELLA *opens the door of the* DOCTOR'S *house.* OTTAVIO *offers his arm to* BEATRICE, FLORINDO *to* ROSAURA, *and in dignified procession they follow the* DOCTOR *into his house.* BRIGHELLA *follows, closing the door. Music stops.*

ARLECCHINO: I don't know what he meant by that, but (*as he sees* COLUMBINA *advancing purposefully upon him*) I do know that, for all the fine tales my master and I have wittily invented, we both seem somehow to have been wittily circumvented.

PANTALONE *remains backstage watching* COLUMBINA *and* ARLECCHINO.

COLUMBINA: Liar! Cheat! Rogue! Humbug!

ARLECCHINO: Eh! How well you know me, my sweet!

COLUMBINA }
ARLECCHINO } (*together*): You fascinating charmer!
You bewitching enchantress!

ARLECCHINO (*aside*): I'm done for!

COLUMBINA: I'm—

ARLECCHINO: I know – you're hungry and you don't want to hear any more of *my* lies until you've had a good meal.

COLUMBINA: After which – you will insist on telling me the truth!

ARLECCHINO (*laughing*): And you'll never believe me!
They go arm in arm into the Inn.

PANTALONE (*coming forward*): If I'm not mistaken, *that* young lady knows how to handle *him* as well.
Music begins again softly. PANTALONE *looks at the Inn door and then turns towards his own door – become suddenly a dejected, lonely old man. The music suddenly increases in volume as out of the Inn come* CLEONICE *and* COLUMBINA. *They seize* PANTALONE *by the arms and lead him towards the Inn door. He resists and as they reach the door he frees himself and – the music softening – he turns to the audience.*

PANTALONE: I was right. They *do* know how to handle them!
Loud music as they seize him again and take him with them into the Inn.

QUICK CURTAIN